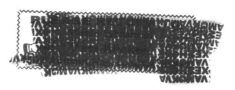

Journey Down The Kreisler Highway

Reflections on the teachings
of Shinichi Suzuki

D0761688

by

Craig Timmerman

Ivory Palaces Music 3141 Spottswood Ave. Memphis, TN 38111

Journey Down The Kreisler Highway
by Craig Timmerman

Editor: Joseph McSpadden
Photographs: Arthur Montzka (p. 3, 10, 63, 92)
              Craig Timmerman (p. 21, 29, 45, 78, 103, cover)
              Ann Schoelles (back cover)
Illustrations: Tom Maxwell, Anita Rodgers
Cover Design: Anita Rodgers
Printing: Diamond Printing

Library of Congress Cataloging in Publication Data

Timmerman, Craig, 1948-
    Journey Down the Kreisler Highway.
    1. Suzuki, Shin'ichi, 1898- . I. Title.
ML418.S83T55 1987   787.1'092'4   87–17326
ISBN 0–943644–07–0

10 9 8 7 6 5 4 3 2

To order this book directly from the publisher, please include payment of $8.95 per book plus $2.00 shipping and handling per order. Foreign air mail surcharge: $5.00 per book.

Foreword

This book began as a series of newsletters written for my students and their parents over a period of 10 years. Within that time many people gave me much help and support in my life and work. I would like to thank them, especially Cathy, Rodney, Julie, Edie, Ethel, Kay, Valery and Carol, Don, Lloyd, Megan, Claire, Christophe and Judy, Lynn, Ruth and Tom, Yuko-San, Yuki-San, Anita, Terry, Diana, and Francoise.

I would also like to thank Dr. Suzuki, Toshio Nakagaki, Art Montzka, the Talent Education Institute, Pantheon Books and Exposition Press for their kind permission to use copyrighted material. Special thanks go to my editor, Joe McSpadden, and the folks at Ivory Palaces, Jack, Phyllis and Jessie, for their insight and encouragement. Thanks also to Kay Slone, Cathy McGlasson, Catherine Cockrill, Julie Parker, Julie Perry, Christine McRae and Allen Lieb for proofreading the text.

As you read, you may wonder about the sequence of chapters, how one leads to the next. Each chapter represents a self-contained letter, and except for the prologue, which explains what the book is about, they are presented pretty much in chronological order.

What I personally find most interesting is the growth being prompted in me by the people and events around me. I sometimes feel as though I would like to go back and experience the whole process again; then I laugh, realizing that I have begun a journey in which there are new experiences just waiting around the next corner.

Craig Timmerman
Lexington, Kentucky
May, 1987

CONTENTS

Part One: *Mankato*

Part Two: *Matsumoto*

Part Three: Lexington

This book is dedicated to Yasuo Tabusa.

Prologue: Certain People

When I write, my inspiration often comes from special people I have known, people who have affected me greatly. I write about such people because I have had a recent encounter, or have a strong need for an encounter with such people again. There exists at times in my life a vacuum which can be filled only by the kind of gift that these special people can give. I then write about these encounters, not so much biographically, but rather to encourage others to watch for people that are special, or perhaps, even to be special persons themselves. Everyone can be special at one time or another by giving just the kind of support and help that another person needs.

I have noticed as I get older that something deep inside me, deep in my "center," has not changed at all, but feels the same as it always did. I seem to carry this feeling through life, although there are things that do have an effect on this place — certain insights, deep experiences, pain, and love.

Certain people have very much affected me in my center. These people were so special because I didn't have to do anything to have them accept me. They just accepted me, unconditionally, without any effort on my part. They didn't actually have to say anything, and in fact, none of them ever did. But their acceptance came across nonetheless. I felt I **could** do anything, but I didn't **need** to. These people reached into my center to nourish and cherish what was already there.

From my childhood I can vividly remember a family neighbor. He was a white-haired football coach who had retired and moved into our neighborhood with his wife. The color of their house was a soft yellow, and that suited them well. They were people who touched the center of every child that came into contact with them. They were interested in so many things around them that they caused my interest to grow. To my knowledge, they never scolded anyone. There was never any need to. What child would misbehave when being nurtured so fully? When I think of these people, I can feel the warmth of their house, though now the color has changed to golden.

I can look back on my life and recall other instances when I have had such powerful experiences. At these times I remember feeling whole and at peace. I can see the person's face and remember my feelings. Sometimes I need those remembrances to carry me through hard times. Other times I just need the glow that is kindled in me.

Two of the people who have so touched the center of my life live in Matsumoto, Japan. They have both devoted their lives to reaching out to the center place within people and providing nourishment and refreshment in their special ways. They teach in different fields, and each uses a different medium for touching people. I was fortunate to receive this special kind of nourishment from each of them almost daily for the year that I lived in this small city in Japan. I truly feel that I have been nurtured by love.

Although not everyone is able to put all else aside and relocate close to a person who can nurture with love like this, there are special people everywhere who nurture in this special way to some degree. Watch for them, and watch them touch. You too may accidentally be nourished and touched.

I wonder what would happen to a child if an adult in his life nourished this kind of flame regularly, so that before the child's flame had a chance to die out, it was rekindled. Then I think about how the child would glow, and how that glow would spread to others. This child would still have to experience pain and difficult times. But always he would have this flame to nurture him and carry with him. What kind of child would he be? What kind of adult would he become?

I wonder too what kind of person would be able to do this for children. I sometimes wonder if such a person couldn't even spark adults! I wonder how some people can get this message across in the way they say the alphabet, or while paying for their groceries, or in a hug.

Then I wonder if this couldn't come across through music — perhaps even in a music lesson . . .

The Heritage You Give Your Children

As Suzuki parents, you are giving your children some special things that they will never forget. I would like to point out a few. Sometimes remembering them can help you through times of struggle with home practice.

I am going to ignore one of the most important gifts you are giving your children, the gift of music. I think everyone has thought a great deal about the enjoyment and growth that come from music. I shall also ignore the way we all work together for the children's self-image and confidence. Instead I am going to discuss some things that are not often talked of, and perhaps seldom thought of, but are truly wonderful gifts.

At some point in each of our lives the time comes when we try to run away from our surroundings, or perhaps even ourselves. There are some things, though, that we cannot get away from, like what is in our heads. Your children will always carry the memory of your working with them each day of their childhood. Can you imagine the warm memory that will be theirs to carry around in later years when they leave home? That memory and knowledge will provide a security and appreciation that will be deeply rooted.

Perhaps, as your children grow older, and their time becomes as valuable as yours is now, they will begin to appreciate even more the difficulties that you had to overcome each day, and your commitment to them to make the effort to overcome those problems. It seems that there is always a special bond within families who give this kind of gift to their children. Undoubtedly it will take years for your children to fully appreciate the gift you have given them, but when that realization does come, what strength it will have.

Perhaps less obvious, but equally important for their later years, will be the daily discipline they will have learned. Your children will always have the advantage and strength of daily discipline as they grow. Music practice is merely the medium; daily discipline in any form gives power to the learning capabilities. You provide this as an outside force in your child's life, knowing that no really great thing can be accomplished without daily discipline. What stability and solidness this gives them!

I rejoice to know that the people that I work with each day are giving so much to their children. They are concerned about the inner growth of their children. What a privilege and joy to be able to work with parents who are so willing to give.

Your Words Are Magic

The more I learn from teaching, the more I value parents and what they say and do. I don't understand it all, but I am beginning to see and learn what Suzuki means by "creating the whole environment."

Let me tell you something I have observed in my years of teaching. Invariably, when a parent talks of a child's behavior within the child's hearing, two things happen:

1. No matter how rambunctiously a child behaves, when a parent starts to talk and says something like, "Johnny is so restless; I can't keep his attention . . .", the child stops whatever he has been doing, grows quiet, and soaks in whatever the parent has been saying.

2. Then, when the parent has finished talking, Johnny reinforces the expected behavior. The parents are always right! The child does exactly what has been described. It never fails. I don't know which comes first, the behavior or the parent's talking, but I know that as long as the parent continues to "explain" her child, that image grows in the child's mind and the behavior pattern becomes more and more complete.

Parents continually plant seeds of behavior in their children. These seeds affect not only the children but also the environment, because now the implanted behavior is expected also by other people. These expectations, like water, fertilizer and sunshine, help that seed to grow healthy and strong into whatever behavior the parents planted.

Parents sometimes say at the lesson, "Amy can't do this; she's never done it before." A seed of defeat is planted. That is why we use the magic weed killer words, "I'll try!" I hope seeds of success are planted along these lines also at home. If you tell me, "Bertha is too shy to play at group lessons," I'll believe you. But I won't blame Bertha. Many experienced teachers don't want to hear anything about the student in advance. It gives the teacher only the best expectations of the child, and the child can let the seeds of goodness grow more easily.

Have you noticed that we often speak of having "a good ear," "a good brain for music," "good memory," "good tone," "good concentration?" We plant these seeds at lessons, at demonstrations in public, after a solo, every chance we get. This is no accident or cute idea. These are seeds that can grow in a child's fertile mind. These good seeds can grow as fast as weeds if they are nurtured by love.

Here is a little experiment you may like to try. Instead of saying peaceful words, say things like, "Don't have a noisy brain!", "Don't have jumpy feet!", "Don't wiggle and fidget!" The brain has an odd habit. It picks out the important words: **noisy, jumpy, wiggle, fidget**. No matter how you construct the sentence, the brain hears it this way. That is why good teachers say things like, "Your brain is getting quiet," or "Your fingers are getting still," with a quiet voice and a quiet mind. See the words the brain picks out now?

Your words are magic! Are they bad magic or good magic?

Heavy Responsibility

Not long ago I was asked to give a lecture at a workshop. I was used to panel discussions, so did not hesitate to agree. However, when I got the schedule, I found that I was to give the lecture by myself. Sure that there had been a mistake, I checked with the person in charge. She said, "Hmmm, That is rather strange, but I'm afraid it's too late to change now." I thought I caught a mischievous smile cross her face, but it could have been the flickering light.

I resigned myself, and in rare spare moments thought about the topic: "The Role and Responsibility of a Suzuki Parent." For

a while I was rather annoyed, because this is just the kind of topic
I like to steer clear of. But gradually I began to form ideas that I
could shape into a lecture on how parents could help their
children learn more, play better, and become better people. I had
faint memories of the many schools of thought on raising
children, and the many books I had studied in earlier days.

When the day of the lecture arrived, I happened upon my
friend in charge, and she asked me how the lecture would go. It
must have been dusty, for she kept winking her eye to clear the
dust out.

I got to the room, sat down, got out my notes, then took time
to relax a bit and look around the room as the parents gathered.
At first I thought I just sensed their exhaustion. But the more I
looked, the more I was convinced that here was a room full of
parents who had heard so many theories about raising children
that they were weighed down by it all. I could see in their faces
that they felt, "Here is just one more person who is going to tell
us how to raise our kids, then say 'Good-bye, see you next year!' "
It became brilliantly clear to me that these parents needed
another lecture on responsibility about as much as I needed to
carry an anvil around in my violin case.

I stood up, piled my notes together, and prepared to
announce, "This lecture is cancelled because of an excess," when
I had an insight. I sat down again and began to speak. Here is
what I said:

"I have read many books about raising children. I have
studied many ideas on the discipline of children. I have watched
parents become convinced of one theory and try it with all their
abilities. I have seen trouble develop, the parents feel a sense of
failure, abandon the old theory and move on to a new one. I have
seen parents who wanted to be such good parents that they
studied whatever they could find written on the topic. And I have
seen them get confused, because there are as many theories as
there are books. They all claim to be right, and they all conflict
with each other. I have seen parents listen to people telling them
how to be better parents, and indeed, I have done that myself.
And I see the effect of all this on your faces here and now. The
role you are asked to play, and the responsibility you are asked to
carry is so heavy, that to carry it at all, you must give up enjoying

your children and pay attention to all these other things.

"I am sure that everything you and I have read has some merit. Some of it might even be helpful. But I think it would be good for all of you to take a rest from your roles and responsibilities for just a little while, long enough to just plain enjoy your children.

"Perhaps, while you are enjoying them, you will come to understand some deep things about them — things like how important it is to hug a child, or what catches and holds the interest of your child. Maybe you will discern things like the moment just before a child loses interest in something. You might be able to perceive the remarkable way in which children learn. You might be astonished at the scope of things children learn by osmosis, perhaps even things we had hoped they might not be noticing. You might even see their astonishing capabilities at manipulating adults in ways that scientists and psychologists are just now starting to discover. You might find out all sorts of amazing tidbits, and enjoy your children as the creations they are.

"There is the possibility that you might find that no one needs to tell you how to be parents at all. You might see that it is possible to discover your own ways, from your own children, and accidentally enjoy your children in new ways. And if nothing else comes of it, at least you will have had a short rest from all the weight and responsibility that has been placed on you. If you discover something that works for your child, don't write another book about it. There are already enough books and theories to confound any sane person."

I tried to end with that, but someone in the room raised his hand and said, "Have you read . . . ?"

Enjoyment Of Our Music

We all know that there is no infallible method to get children to practice regularly. There is one word, though, that will help us a great deal, and that word is "enjoy."

We all like to do what is enjoyable, and we do not want to do what is not enjoyable. We may even go to some effort to avoid doing an unenjoyable task. As adults we know that we must sometimes do things that we do not enjoy, even though we may dread the task for days ahead of time.

Let us think of the children now. Do they, and really, can they enjoy their practice? As adults in control of the situation, we know that if we don't enjoy the lesson there is no way the child is going to enjoy it either. If at home the practice is hurriedly crammed into some "extra time" during the day, all the people involved will feel the pressure created by this problem situation.

For the older, school-age children, with routines and schedules already programmed in their lives, a practice schedule may help both the parent and the child. On the other hand, because of routines already in the child's life, a less rigid format may be necessary. Schedule or not, if the home practice period has pressure on it, the enjoyment will be much less for everyone involved.

For preschool children, much more awareness is needed from the parent. A specific daily practice time of set length rarely works well or gives joy to the young child. The parent must be aware of the right opportunities that come up during the day — five minutes here and five minutes there — when the child is in a learning mood.

You might begin by singing a piece or two from the record, not "aiming" it at the child, but so that the child can sense that you enjoy these pieces too. This can be done in the car, while doing chores around the house, or at many other times in your daily routine. Such activities make the whole day a joyful practice or learning time. It takes much creativity on the parent's part, but creativity enhances joy.

Do you talk about music with your child? Listen to records or concerts? Talk of the good time had during lessons or group lessons? These things, which seem unrelated to practice, can set the tone in the child's mind about his own talent, his instrument, and music in general.

Encourage spontaneous sessions with your child, for these reveal the child's enthusiasm for music and joy in learning. It is very important that you not do any correcting at these times. Find something to compliment, and be sure to tell him what he is doing correctly.

Another small thing that you can do to enhance enjoyment is to prepare your child psychologically before and after the lesson. You might ask your child, "I wonder if your teacher will notice how fine your position is today?", or "I remember how good your tone was at your last lesson." After the lesson use the same kinds of positive statements.

All these things can help keep the child's attitude, and your own, ready to enjoy the music that the child is making. Not only will it help to make practice enjoyable but much more effective also. If we don't enjoy our own music and the skills we are developing, of what good is our music?

Part Of Life

Recently a parent told me, "You treat my child like your own grandchild." I didn't catch her point, so she went on to make it more obvious: "As parents, we often don't have the time to really appreciate our children; we are caught up in all the other things happening. But it seems that grandparents take the time to hear what children want to tell them, to hold them on their laps, and give them all the hugs that they can hold. I think that if I could approach the lessons at home more like a grandparent, things might have more joy in them."

After she told me this, I began to study grandparents with children. It is a treat to behold. They are so proud of these children, and so happy just to have them around! Children seem to glow in the presence of their grandparents. Since then, I have often thought of approaching children like a grandparent too.

Recently I have thought a great deal about my own grandmother. She was such a good grandmotherly type, and she was grandmotherly to everyone; but to her own grandchildren she was something more. She always had an abundance of praises for each of her grandchildren. She would use them in our presence, but even more important, she would praise us when we weren't even around. We always tried to act embarrassed when she told others of our good points or successes, but she always knew how good it made us feel.

She had some wonderful ways about her. One of them was her sense of teasing: she knew just how much was good. Shortly after her 82nd birthday, while spraying her flowers with a plant mister, she said to me, "Craig, you tease people too much." With that, she sprayed me full in the face. I can still hear her laughing as I sputtered and stammered. Thereafter, knowing me very well, she always hid the sprayer whenever I came to her house.

Until she was 80 she walked to the corner grocery and carried her groceries home. However, after her heart attack she would often ride to the store with me. In the winter time, on the way home I would usually find an icy parking lot or deserted street and go skidding and sliding around turns. She always pretended to be frightened, but she knew how much I liked this little game.

She would get in the car and say, "Now, no spinning today. My heart won't take it." Then she would try to hide her smile and sparkling eyes. She was a little like the playful Br'er Rabbit, I think.

Recently her family was gathered around her again. Her love was still strong, her faith inspiring. We were all a bit sad, but for Grandma it was her day of glory. She drew her family together in a way that was stronger than ever before, and she taught us about love, support, and tears.

She had asked me for years to play the hymn "What A Friend We Have In Jesus" at her rising day. As her casket was being lowered into the ground I played, under the sky, as her family tried to sing. I know Grandma heard us and tried to comfort us as her song was carried away by the gentle breeze.

Afterward, we went back to share food at her church. Suddenly a hobo appeared, a total stranger, asking for a free lunch at Grandma's funeral dinner. I was aghast, and was about to send him away. But her children interceded saying, "This is a special reminder of Grandma for us." They then told me that, during the Depression, some hobo or other would come to her house every day to ask for food. Often Grandma would invite the man in to have supper with the family. But if he was too dirty, or wouldn't come in, she would have one of her children eat on the back porch with him. Often Grandma had only a loaf of bread to feed her own family. But no matter what she had, she shared. It turned out that this hobo was the guest of honor at the dinner.

Grandma always went by her own rules and managed her own affairs. She claimed to have special prayer connections to God, and I believe she did. Grandma taught me a great deal about teaching, about giving, about helping other people feel good, and about love.

I Am Underwhelmed

Several years ago I began to search for teaching methods that really affect people wholly. I began to look for powerful ways to transmit to others what I thought was important. At various institutes I began to watch teachers with this goal in mind. I saw teachers who had a great deal of power and dynamism in their approach. I also saw children controlled, and therefore thought that great things were happening. I looked for powerful tricks and methods.

I was lucky enough to observe some of the finest teachers in the country. At my first observation of a very renowned teacher, I nearly fell asleep and rolled off my chair. As I struggled to keep awake, I thought to myself, "My goodness, he had better get some action going, or these kids are going to fall asleep too!" I was able to get through the lesson without falling off my chair, but luckily, I was sitting in an armchair.

I felt I ought to go back the next day, because I knew that such a renowned teacher could not be so highly thought of by accident. I resolved to drink a lot of coffee before the lesson and try to observe more of what was happening to the children. Again, I began to get drowsy because of what seemed to be complete lethargy in the proceedings.

By chance, though, I happened to think, "This lesson isn't meant for the audience. It is for the children. Perhaps I should try to see what is happening in the students instead of in me." The drowsiness left me immediately. The students were very relaxed, participating, and learning an immense amount, freely, joyfully, and at their own speed. This teacher was so relaxed and unforcing that the students were learning completely without fear.

After watching other teachers, I could see that a teacher who teaches from this viewpoint can engender a wonderful freedom and responsiveness in the children. I also observed that most parents were fooled as greatly as I by an "underwhelming" teacher. I hope my experience encourages parents to observe what happens in their children when they work with a teacher, not what happens to the parent.

I know there is more to good teaching than mere "underwhelming," for in experimenting, I have found that underwhelming alone will not make a good teacher. I also have found that there are many very fine teachers who teach with great dynamic force and energy, and there, too, the students grow and learn. "Underwhelming" is not the only answer, nor is "overwhelming." But I hope that as you work with various teachers, you will look for the growth that takes place in the child. Don't be fooled, as I was. You may not be lucky enough to get a chair with arms on it.

Teaching Power

As I left Mankato for a week of observation and study, I thought that I might find "teaching power." To my surprise, I found that one cannot really "teach" another person at all!

Most of us were taught by the "force-feed" method, and we still have people trying to teach in that way. Perhaps you have heard the wise old saying, "A man persuaded against his will is of the same opinion still." This says a great deal about teaching. Whenever we try to exert enough pressure on a child to change him or "teach" him, we invoke the physical law: "To every action there is an equal and opposite reaction."

I have come to believe that a special environment, plus acceptance, will produce growth in a child. I have seen teachers teach with this formula and observed the results. The students are free to grow and bloom with joy and sensitivity. This explains why some teachers can be so effective as "underwhelmers" and others, with great dynamism, can be equally effective. I say, "Do not scold a child. Instead, show him love and acceptance, and provide him with everything he needs to freely change his playing." Teachers must respect their students, for if a teacher respects the student at his level, the child will not fear for loss of pride or place, and thus is free to grow. Once the student is given this freedom, we teachers must be sure to provide correct examples. Once a child is freed this way, he will learn very quickly whatever is around him.

Here Comes The Judge

I have had the privilege of knowing a number of people

whom I consider to be "great" people. They possess a talent recognized by many others, yet they all have one quality which, to me, is what makes them really great. These people have so much to offer and teach to everyone around them, yet they somehow never give the impression that they feel superior. On the contrary, they are genuinely humble.

Their humility, however, seems to come from an unusual source, for these people are completely non-judgmental. They can teach, help, live and breathe, and there is never any judgment involved. It is a quality that I revere and look for. The feeling of freedom that comes from being in the presence of such a person is hard to explain unless one has actually experienced it. But once you have felt it you won't ever forget the feeling; you feel free to grow in the presence of this person.

I have seen some very renowned teachers make such biting judgments toward their students that the students became unable to learn or perform at anywhere near a normal level. In such situations some students just aren't capable of standing up to the pressure and the judgments constantly being made by the teacher. These students drop out and are often labeled as "failures".

Suzuki says, "Everyone can be educated." If a teacher approaches a student with this philosophy, there can be a wholly different attitude in the student. I think that one of the most important qualities that a teacher can have is knowing that every person can be educated, but at that individual's rate of learning. Instead of judging a student, or any person, we should look for that person's "living soul".

I am so happy that I know people who approach others in this manner. They are scattered around the world. But wherever they are, people begin to blossom around them. Contact with "living soul" helps every person to bloom freely as a full and beautiful flower.

I was once told by a person of this calibre, "Don't try to teach students, just love them." Well, that is a very odd statement coming from a renowned teacher, and I thought, "My goodness, if I am supposed to be a teacher, I had better 'teach'." But as I tried this idea, I found that the students were able to soak up what I had to offer and were growing freely. As so many students began to bloom right before my eyes, I became convinced that if I look for the "living soul" in each child, no one will say as I walk into a room, "Here comes the judge."

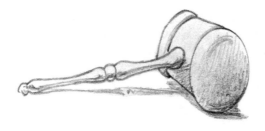

Not In This Town, There Ain't

There is an old saying that goes, "An expert never lives in this town, and the farther away an expert lives, the more of an expert he is." Sounds silly, doesn't it? This saying is neither good nor bad, but it is true. What is familiar to us begins to lose significance. What is less familiar has more of an impact on us.

It is easy to see that lessons with the teacher are always different from home lessons with the parent, though not always better. Soon, however, the child begins to have room for experiences even beyond lessons with the teacher. This "beyond" is what I speak of now.

Someone once said to me, "Anything significant that has happened to me, has happened either during, or as a direct result of, an island experience." By "island experience" he meant an experience set aside, out of the ordinary.

This idea is important for two reasons. First, it helps me put into better perspective the teaching I do with my own students. Second, it motivates me to create island experiences for the students, and to encourage students and parents to participate in such things.

I feel a need to point out here that we strive not only for quality in music, but also for quality in people. There are people all over the world, joined together by music and by Suzuki himself, who are working for these qualities, so that we are able to draw upon a vast reservoir of human resources. Most out-of-town activities, visits by guest teachers, workshops and institutes are set up for this very purpose.

Reflecting on these ideas, I have begun to see my role in a much different light. I now feel that my job is to give students a good foundation so that they are prepared to obtain the most benefit from an island experience. To give them a solid base, technically and musically, from which to start is important. But even more important is to prepare the students to be able to respect and learn from an island experience.

It may sound like I am relieving myself of a great deal of responsibility when I say this, but I think not. Children as people are most important. Music and growth will come as the children are prepared for them. We cannot really teach anything; we can only open the door for the children to learn and develop ability.

For these reasons I encourage island experiences in order that you and your children have special opportunities for growth, not just in music, but in any discipline.

Do you know any expert in your town?

Changing Ideas Inspired By An Institute

As a teacher I am constantly giving out what I have soaked in. At times I feel like a well run dry, and need to be filled up again so that I may have more to give. I have just come back from an Institute with Dr. Suzuki, and am bursting with inspiration and ideas for my students. The first broad area that I am thinking about is practice as a result of a musical environment. If we think of practice in "minutes per day", we do an injustice to our children. We should fill our homes with music all day long, so that practice will fit into the environment and not be something just tacked on. How can parents think of the recordings not as listening assignments, but as music for themselves to enjoy? By learning the pieces, humming the tunes, feeling the beat of the music, not as a trick to get the child involved, but as a joy and pleasure in their own lives. Then it cannot help but spill over into the lives of the children. Suzuki used to say that listening is as important as practice. He has stopped saying that. He now says that listening is twice as important as practice!

Another point that stretches my mind is Suzuki's belief that ability grows at home, and that we develop ability by perfecting pieces we already know, not by moving on to the next piece. As he said this during a lecture, I felt inspired and excited. We would become free to learn music, not just notes and bowings. If we were not always bogged down at lessons by those things that could have been learned by repetition, then we would have something left for musicality!

A suggestion that came up many times was never to discuss a

child's problematic behavior when the child is around. Suzuki's
reason is that when the child hears important adults talk about
such a problem, the difficulty is thereby reinforced in the child.
As I thought about this, the essence of it seemed to be that we are
belittling a person's importance when we discuss their problems
in their presence. Whether it is a child who won't understand our
sophisticated vocabulary or a deaf person who can't understand a
word we say, we are doing something unkind to the spirit of that
person. Since we are trying to raise the self-esteem of these
children, let us affirm their presence whenever we can.

Last Thoughts Before Leaving For Japan

What am I leaving behind? The first thing that comes to
mind is people — my family, students, their families, friends. As I
think of leaving these people, I ask myself, "In what way am I
leaving them?" I am really leaving only my physical interaction
with them. I will not be able to do things with these people, in a
physical sense, for a year. But, I will be able to do things with
new people that I meet where I go. So this loss of physically
being present really isn't very great.

What is truly important about these people I am leaving is
their love for me, and my love for them. The wonderful thing
about love is that it has no distance barriers; whether I am in
Mankato or Japan, there is no difference in the love that can be
spiritually communicated. I am not leaving love behind at all.
My suitcase is filled with it. Certainly my love for the people at
home is as great as ever.

What am I heading toward? There are many questions
inherent in this one question, but they cannot be answered until I
arrive in Japan. What one person experiences in certain surroundings, another experiences quite differently. I know that the
country is very beautiful around Matsumoto. I know that the
culture will be very different. I know that it will be strange to be a
student again, after teaching for ten years. I know that being in
the presence of Dr. Suzuki and many other fine human beings

will be a great inspiration. I know that being surrounded by so many fine students, and so much good music, will help me to grow musically a great deal. But I can't really say what I am heading toward. I can only answer to what is happening now, and what I am experiencing now. I could answer by relating experiences others have had in Japan, but that may not even be close to what I will have. So the only real answer to that question is, "Wait and see!"

What excites me most is the realization that I will be able to experience, as a student, the kind of environment I have been trying to create for my students at home. This is my greatest motivation for going to Japan. I have felt for years that the environment is vitally important for children and families. Now, I will be able to live in the ideal environment as a student.

My New Understanding
Of The "Mother Tongue" Approach

For ten years I taught with my understanding of the "Mother Tongue" approach. Many times in those years I received insights into this idea. However, I never had the chance to experience it as an infant would. Now the reality of the greatness inherent in this method has struck me.

I have arrived in a foreign land, where I rarely hear a word uttered that I understand, where actions and body language speak differently from what I am used to, and where most of what I do doesn't make sense to the people here. I am now beginning to understand how the one-year-old operates.

I hear sounds uttered all around me that don't make sense. Certain sounds that I hear very often begin to sound familiar. I perk up my ear whenever I hear a sound that I know. Sometimes I make the effort to make this same sound. People all around me stop what they are doing and show me great signs of encouragement. This makes me want to keep saying the same word over many times. I really enjoy the repetition of a word for which I have gained positive reinforcement.

When I don't get to repeat a new word enough I get frustrated and confused. It takes all the fun away. I need to feel really confident with each new word and enjoy it fully. Otherwise, I get unsure of what I already know.

Sometimes the people around me let me repeat the word enough to really enjoy it. But more often, when people see that I am learning new words they get excited. They think, "Oh good. Now we can teach you a whole bunch." Then I get "sat down" and "taught at", and a whole rash of new words and grammatical explanations start in my mind and mix up the words that are already there.

Well really! Not only does this bore me, because I'm not interested in sentence structure and grammatical rules, but it is also way over my head. I start to get irritated and annoyed, even though people try to teach me with the best of intentions. I have found some delightful ways to change the subject, and then laugh at myself when I remember a child doing the same thing to me when I tried to "teach" her.

I never get bored otherwise, because everything is so wonderfully new and interesting. Because it is mostly unconscious learning, which happens on a deep level and takes lots of energy, I get worn out quickly and find that I have a short attention span.

In learning the language and the culture, I have seen many foreign people that speak excellent Japanese and understand the body language here. I have even found a pet parrot that speaks better Japanese than I do! But still I haven't lost interest because no one has compared me to someone who is better than I am. I am finding it all enjoyable, interesting, rewarding and exhausting.

I see now that the life of a young child is not easy. But by becoming a two-year-old here, I can certainly better understand the needs of children who are learning. Now Suzuki's parallel of learning a language to playing an instrument becomes clear.

It can be fun to learn as a two year old, but if I am pushed, I know I can't learn. Then I'll come out with the label of being "unteachable".

Soon I shall be three.

The Eyes Of The Man

Dr. Suzuki has a "joke" about his age. He says he is sixteen years old — 7 and 9, after all, are sixteen! However, I think he is wrong. I put his age at closer to four years old. I judge his age by his eyes, and I mean it as a compliment of the highest order to say he is four years old.

Have you ever looked at the eyes of a four-year-old? They are very clear. They are deep and trusting. They shine with a terrific sparkle, a fascination with life, an ability to see everything for the first time, and a certain amount of mischief!

All of these things are in the eyes of this four year old man, along with a huge amount of Love. His eyes never seem to rest. They are always sparkling, searching, loving. And during one of his many jokes they are laughing loudly. I have seen very few people over the age of twenty-five enjoy humor as much as Dr. Suzuki, and he laughs more than most children his age.

He can also laugh until the tears flow without ever laughing **at** anyone or making anyone feel laughed at. Sheer joy makes him laugh. Hearing him laugh and seeing his eyes laugh spreads joy to all who are around. He has some kind of strange talent that I have never observed in anyone else. He can tell the same jokes many times, yet every time he tells those jokes they are so very funny. When he laughs at them it is impossible not to laugh also. I think there is such joy in his heart that everyone around feels it and also laughs with joy.

I saw him do this even in a very dramatic setting. Not long ago, the princess of Japan was in Matsumoto for a celebration of a peace movement that has begun here in Japan. Dr. Suzuki was one of the honored guests, and he made sure that many of the foreign students were invited. At this meeting we foreigners could not understand anything that was being said, so I watched other people very carefully. For nearly three hours speeches were given and various ceremonies were performed. Not once during this time did I see a smile or hear even a small bit of laughter among the several thousand people present. When Dr. Suzuki came on stage, however, he had the whole crowd relaxed and laughing within thirty seconds. There were smiles, laughter, and pure enjoyment floating around the whole place during his presentation. He had the spontaneity of a four-year-old as he spread joy where there had been none.

This four-year-old is the most delightful child I know. I hope that by the time I have reached eighty I will have learned how to be four.

A Personal Letter To My Students In Mankato

Now I know some of the feelings of a VIP, first class. Last week I went to speak to an English class at a Junior High School in a very small town at the top of the mountain near Matsumoto. This town of 4,500 has an excellent school system, as evidenced partly by the buildings, and partly by the fact that the administrators of the school have been to several other countries to observe educational systems and ideas. They are so progressive that they even bring a foreigner to the school to speak. The building was very modern, even by American standards, and the concept of the "open school" was being tried — something very new for Japan.

Getting to this town I went on my first train trip alone in Japan. I was quite nervous as I had to make a transfer, and all of the signs were in Japanese.

Wherever I traveled, Japanese people would come to me and say things in English and ask me to help them with pronunciation. Usually they could not converse, but were just practicing English. So, I thought while on this train trip I might divert myself by practicing Japanese. The phrase that I was striving to pronounce and memorize was, "Please call me a taxi." There was a man sitting across the aisle giving me an occasional furtive glance. I thought he might prove to be helpful, so I studied my phrase diligently, preparing to say it to him. I didn't know how to ask him to help me pronounce it correctly, but I thought he would get the drift of what I was doing.

I looked him in the eye and said, "Please call me a taxi." He looked very confused, so I began giving hand signals so that he would understand that I wanted him to say the same thing to me. But he only looked more confused. I tried again, slower, and a bit louder, giving great hand gestures. He didn't say anything, and I couldn't get him to even try. I had learned by this time that when a Japanese person says, "**Yes!**" in a definitive way, it is almost a command. So I said to him, "Please call me a taxi, **Yes! Yes!**" He said, "Yes," got up, and started walking toward the door. I hadn't noticed until then that the train was stopped at a small local station. The man got off the train and started walking toward a phone booth. I shouted, "**Stop!**" He looked around, hopelessly confused, and I couldn't even begin to explain what he had done wrong. I pointed to our seats. When he got back on the train, we sat down, and I put away my phrase book without uttering another word until we reached the station where I was to get off.

I was met by the English teacher of the school and ushered into the administration office for coffee with the principal and some assistant principals. They couldn't speak English, but they were very kind to me.

After coffee I was shown into the faculty office. All of the teachers of the school have desks in this large room. There were about 20 teachers all sitting at their desks waiting for me to be introduced. It made me wonder who was teaching the students at that moment. Then I was taken to the auditorium, where I found out why the teachers could all be in their office, for the whole student body was seated in this room. They were sitting very quietly, and when I came in there was a rush of excitement. All of the students are required to study English and some history of America and other English-speaking countries. It took a while before it really began to dawn on me, though, how little contact these people had had with foreigners. I spoke a few words in English after I was introduced and the English teacher translated into Japanese. I was told that I should then go to the classroom. As I left the auditorium with the principal, no one else even moved or spoke until I was out of the room.

The English class was a joy to speak to. No one in this class of 7th graders had ever spoken to a foreigner before, let alone in English. They were very excited and eager, but also quite nervous. The teacher told me later that they usually speak in very loud voices, but today they were so nervous that they could hardly be heard. In all the classes the children asked me a few questions in Japanese and the teacher translated the questions and answers. The first question that came up was about my beard. It was somewhat embarrassing to the teachers, but they were just as anxious to know about my beard as the children were. In Japan, usually only very old men have beards, and even then very seldom. One Japanese man guessed my age to be over 50 because of my beard. When I told him I was under 30 he was astonished.

After the class was over, the children came up to shake hands. They seemed extremely nervous about this. Later I found out from the teacher that not only was this the first time they had shaken hands with a foreigner, it was probably the first time in their lives that they had shaken hands at all! When I was busily engaged in shaking hands, a few of the braver students came up and touched my beard and then ran away. It was very funny.

After I finished speaking to the classes I was fed a school lunch, although I have a feeling it might have been a "special." After lunch I was taken downtown where I met the mayor of the city and the school board members. All in all, it was a very interesting day. The train ride back to Matsumoto was very dry, comparatively speaking. You can be assured that I did not practice any Japanese on the way home.

In the first week that I came to Japan there was a religious festival and holiday. This meant that there were huge crowds in the streets having great celebrations. Already in the first week in Japan I had met a great many friendly people, so I knew that someone might want to meet and welcome a new foreigner in town. As I was wandering about in this festive crowd I saw a man coming towards me who looked like he wanted to shake my hand. I thought it was somewhat unusual that he would extend his hand at such a distance from me, but then I assumed that he was inexperienced in hand shaking so really couldn't know the proper way of it all. He kept coming towards me and I extended my hand, but he didn't put his hand where I am used to getting a hand to shake. He just kept going up and down. I tried to match his speed to shake, but he didn't seem to get the idea. Finally, I grabbed his hand with both of mine and shook it properly. I must admit that he did have a very startled expression on his face at the time, but it wasn't until a few days later that I found out what really happened: in crowded conditions, the polite way to cut in front of someone is to make an up and down cutting motion in front of your body with your right hand. It means "excuse me" in nonverbal language. I must admit that the man was very polite under the circumstances, and after I caught his hand and he caught his breath, we shook hands very well.

Some of you who have been in my home in Mankato know that I am a fancier of aquariums and tropical fish. While I had aquariums I became just as fascinated with the plants and the other kinds of life in the tanks as with the fish. At one time I had some beautiful large snails in my tanks. These little creatures were called "mystery snails," and they were delightful little fellows.

It is a custom here that at each meal, including breakfast, we have rice and a soup called *miso* soup. To give this soup a variety, a different item is put in the base each day to give a theme to the flavor, as it were. I had grown accustomed to finding things like sea grass, small fish, onions, and sometimes chicken or pork in the bottom of the opaque soup. One day, however, I was eating my soup with chopsticks and I felt a large, hard lump at the bottom. I couldn't figure out what it was, so I lifted it out of the soup and set it on my tray. I was very startled to see something that looked exactly like my little friend the "mystery snail." It took me several minutes to get over the shock. Then I looked around and found that, yes, everyone else had a snail in their soup too. So I had to call the waitress and ask her to show me how to eat the little fellow. The big trick was not getting him out of the shell, as the waitress thought, but to swallow him once he was in my mouth.

I have mentioned before how it is to be isolated from the news. We can read one or two Japanese papers in English to be sure, but it is very much world news and not much about what is happening in America. If one has a short wave radio, one can hear American news on "The Voice of America," which seems like a wonderful thing to me nowadays. The only problem is that it is often electronically jammed, and part way through the news the voices are obliterated by a horrendous shrill sound that forces one to turn off the radio. Tonight, as I write this letter, my housemate and I are hearing a whole broadcast that hasn't been jammed. It seems like something out of a movie.

The Hammer

The Japanese people have a different way of imparting information than we Westerners. We are used to having things spelled out in a very organized fashion, giving us all the data we need, and requiring little thinking on our part. But Suzuki, I find, gives out little clues here and there, rarely, if ever, giving any answers. As we get closer to something, the excitement builds, and we search even harder. When we are almost at the end of the trail, Suzuki will often give us the final clue, which then hits like a hammer. Suddenly our whole search makes sense, the detours become visible in hindsight, and the concept becomes bright in our minds because of the search and the "hammer". Sometimes it is hard to stay patient while searching, but for me the wait has always been worth the results.

Recently I was impressed by what happened after a concert given here by some of the children. The parents handed each child a folder and the children started unravelling charts from the folders. These are called "Ability Development Charts". Horizontally the pages are marked off in ½ inch squares; vertically they list the pieces in the Suzuki books. Only after the child has mastered a piece well enough to play with the accompaniment tape can he start marking squares on the chart. Each folder lasts one year, and some of the charts were ten feet long! So these children had played pieces they knew very well, with the accompaniment tapes, hundreds of times last year.

While I was still somewhat astonished at the charts, Suzuki came up with the "hammer". He said to me, "**Understanding is not ability. It is knowledge. Practicing 10,000 times with understanding — this makes ability.**"

I Finally Find Out
What "Listening" Means To Suzuki

It seems strange that after years of teaching with the "Suzuki Method", I should find out only now, after more than two months in Japan, what Suzuki really means when he says, "More listening." Only now have I fully understood the significance of proper listening techniques.

Most of us have heard from the Japanese teachers who visit America that if there are any problems connected with the music at all, they can be cured by proper listening. After hearing this mentioned, I stepped up my listening to the Suzuki materials, but still found that I had difficulty memorizing pieces quickly. In the States I had used the idea of recording a difficult piece several times on the same cassette. In this way I could hear the piece several extra times during the day. For children, however, I suggested this only as a "trick."

Last week, I found out from a teacher here what is really meant by "listening" in Japan. It means hearing the pieces, particularly the shorter ones, at least 50 times a day! Well, that was a real shock at first. But after more discussion, I found that, by using the audio machines at our disposal, it was easy to fill a whole side of a tape with one or two pieces and then replay the tape several times throughout the day.

By a strange coincidence, two days after I learned this I was able to test the theory for myself. Suzuki told all the student teachers one day, "Next week we will all play together and study the Bach *Corrente*." He mentioned several points to study in particular. Then we listened to Casals play the piece on a tape.

I must admit that I was in somewhat of a state of shock after this, for my ability to memorize is appallingly slow. For me to memorize a piece in only seven days seemed quite impossible. But I went home and made a special tape of the piece. Then I really began to hear it an hour a day. It is surprising that even now, long after the piece was memorized, I haven't grown tired of hearing the music.

During the times when I actually listened intently I heard the points that Suzuki had emphasized. Of the many times I heard the piece each day, of course, I really only listened closely to it one or two times. But being in the mood to test this theory, for four days I just played the tape as mentioned. Then for three days I practiced that piece about 20 minutes each day. In seven days I had it memorized! For me that is a feat of unequalled proportions, and one that I shall not soon forget. Now, as I practice the piece from memory, I can think of the points that Suzuki talked of, and I get a great deal more out of the piece than would have ever been possible before. This memorization feat has been one of the more pleasant surprises that I have had in Japan, and it is a method I shall use from now on.

I realize that as my memory develops by using this technique, memorization will become even easier. Suzuki has played several tricks on me to emphasize this very thing. More than once he has called me into his studio to watch a particular lesson. He teaches very few children now in Japan (he teaches mostly teachers), so I was delighted to watch him teach some children.

The first time he tricked me, he was teaching a girl of about twelve who was playing the Bach "*Chaconne* in D minor" (from memory, of course). This piece, which takes about 20 minutes to play, is considered one of the most difficult works for the violin, both technically and musically. Actually, I was somewhat disappointed. She played rather roughly and unmusically. Suzuki worked on some points with her, and she improved vastly during the lesson. He said to me after her lesson, "A difficult piece, no?" I said, "Yes." Then, with that special twinkle in his eyes, he dropped the hammer: "Yes, two weeks ago I asked her to prepare this piece."

Suzuki is really very good at setting traps like these to teach a certain point. He does it with such humor and wit that sometimes I leave the school with a sore side from laughing so hard. He always baits the hook just right, and I always take the bait hook, line and sinker. It makes learning so exciting.

But.. But.. But..

I have heard so many objections to the use of the Japanese accompaniment tapes that I could not count them all. At one time I thought that these objections were logical and valid. Now, however, I think the tapes, used properly, are the most important environmental teaching aid I have found in Japan. By "environmental aid," I mean the kind of aid that teaches by osmosis, not by explanation. I have noticed how the Japanese teachers use environmental aids to multiply learning effectiveness. Please notice that I said, "multiply," not "add to" the effectiveness.

One of the benefits of the tapes is to teach musical movement. Indeed, somehow we must learn that music actually has movement and is not just made from notes. Without musical movement we can hear only notes.

It would be absurd to expound on this theory to children, for not only would they not understand the theory, but the explanation wouldn't help them understand movement. They must actually experience it, and often enough that it becomes a part of them.

There are many nuances of movement in the accompaniment tapes, even in "Book One." Some of the nuances I don't agree with, but all the better! They are places that make me acutely aware of the piece's movement. If we are riding along in a car, after a while we do not even notice that we are moving. We might read a book as if we were in our living room. But, should the car suddenly swerve or stop, we become instantly aware that we are moving.

The tapes move along fast enough so that we cannot get stuck in the notes. We must learn the piece well enough that we can get above the notes and find the music, the movement, and the life. It all starts with the first variation of "Twinkle."

A second benefit is tied closely to the first. That is, unlike a good accompanist, these tapes don't follow the student. They cannot slow down in the hard passages, or speed up in the easy ones, or drift from tempo to tempo. This point was brought home to me by a very funny lesson from Suzuki.

At one group lesson Suzuki had all the teacher trainees play "*La Folia*" with the best accompanist at the Institute. Soon, Suzuki began to laugh. The pianist was very skillful in catching the tempo from the violinists, and since every person was playing his own best rendition of "*La Folia*," there were 30 different versions, actually 31 counting the pianist's. Still chuckling, Suzuki said, "Next week we play with a tape! It cannot follow you." To my surprise, the next week there was only one version of the piece. We were unified. And, there was one very relieved pianist.

A musician must have an individual musical "sense" that an accompanist can follow. This sense must be developed; it is not just "there" in the young student. To let a child play at an undisciplined tempo, no matter how expressively, will not develop musical sensitivity.

"Musical Movement" is one of Suzuki's pet ideas at this time, and he is currently doing studies on this idea so that students can develop an awareness of movement in music. He is preparing tapes for the students to move with in rhythm in a style he calls "conducting".

A disadvantage to the tapes is the matter of pitch. No two tape recorders will reproduce exactly the same pitch, so it is a very difficult problem. The dreadfulness of the situation was made clear when I asked a class of students to play the Vivaldi "A minor Concerto". I turned on the tape and they began playing. I was aghast. The pitch was a quarter step high. Turning to the students to see their reaction, I was astonished. They didn't show the least bit of surprise or annoyance. They simply played in tune with the tape at its own pitch. The only times they were out of tune was when they played open strings. I stopped the tape and stared at them with my mouth agape. They hadn't realized that they had done anything unusual, and were somewhat annoyed at me for stopping to point out something so normal. I couldn't even impress the parents with what their children had done. I remained the only astonished one in the class.

The most forceful argument for the use of accompaniment tapes is that they provide a wonderful performance standard. In Japan, children study a piece until they are able to play it with the tape beautifully. Then they bring the tape to the lesson and play with the tape for the teacher. If they are successful, they then start to study musicality on that piece while beginning to study the next piece, for which they, of course, have already done preliminary exercises. The student and parent know what and how to practice to bring the piece to life.

I could write many pages about the importance of the use of these multipliers, but really the theory does not help much. When a person starts to use the tapes the results will shout loudly enough for anyone to catch.

This Teacher's Students Will Be Advanced

Suzuki begins every lesson with tonalization. In fact, almost every lesson is at least one-half tonalization. Even the most advanced students study tone production with Suzuki. One day Suzuki had a talk with me and said something of utmost importance for every teacher and student of music. He said, "If the teacher can teach tonalization, then the students will become advanced and play from the heart." I know an old *Zen* story that helps explain Suzuki's meaning.

A young boy went to a *Zen* master to learn about the precious jade stone. The first day the boy went, the master pressed a small round piece of jade into the young fellow's hand. He then proceeded to talk at length about the wind. After a time the master said, "The lesson for today is over." The boy gave the jade back to the master and went home.

This same process continued for many weeks. Every day the master pressed a jade stone in to the boy's hand, closed the young fellow's fingers around the stone and began to talk of many things of life.

One day the boy's parents asked him, "What are you learning about jade from the *Zen* master?" The boy became confused for a moment, for he had forgotten that he was to study about jade. He had become so engrossed in what the master was telling him about nature that he hadn't become concerned until he was reminded about his "real" reason for study. The boy decided that today he would have to remind the master that his purpose was to study jade, and so he must get on with the "real" lessons.

The boy went with his intention firmly in mind. When he got to his lesson, the master put a small round stone in his hand and closed his fingers around it. All of a sudden the boy jumped to his feet and shouted, "This is not jade!"

If you can see the connection between "nature" and "jade," then I think you can see the way in which the master was teaching the boy. In many ways this seems to be how Suzuki teaches us. If I can trust my teacher enough and be patient, then what he has to offer will gradually become a part of me without any struggle. As soon as doubt enters my mind about what Suzuki is doing, I miss the whole point of my lesson.

This story has helped me understand many things, including the connection between "tonalization" and "playing from the heart". Suzuki teaches the technique of making sound that can transmit subtle feelings from inside us. If I look only at the exercises he gives in the tonalization studies each lesson, they seem almost nonsensical. But if I am patient, all of a sudden someone might stand up when I play and say, "This is heart-tone!"

Where Is Suzuki?

I have seen things recently that make me wonder how high or low Suzuki is. Just where is his level? Suzuki seems to consider all people to be of incredible value. He can be meeting with a world famous artist one minute, and yet, if one of his students comes to him with a need, Suzuki takes care of that need. He treats everyone with true respect. I think everyone he comes in contact with can feel this, and it lifts our spirits to new heights.

Here we have one of the greatest teachers in the world, one of the greatest human beings. Yet, one day, during my lesson I dropped my cassette tape on the floor, and before I could pick it up, Suzuki had taken several steps, picked it up and handed it to me. That may be one of the most significant violin lessons I'll ever receive.

One day during a recital here, the pianist needed a page

turner. Can you guess who was the first one on stage to help her?

Sometimes during a lesson Suzuki will suddenly start jumping crazily around the room. Then he will say to one of us, "Now we have a contest. Who can jump the farthest?" He will make a good jump and then say to the other contestant, "You must not bend your legs before you jump. If you want to play the violin without preparation, then you must jump without preparation."

I have always been laughing too hard to see who wins the contest, but I can well imagine. I suppose it is a good way to get a point across, but I wonder if such an important person should be acting so undignified.

One day when I began to realize "where Suzuki was," I decided to see if I was wrong about my thinking, so I devised a test of my own. Dr. Suzuki has a very special chair that was given to him by the teachers in Japan. He is able to completely relax in this chair during the time he actually sits down while teaching. One day during a lesson, just after he had jumped out of his chair to help a student, I sneaked over and sat in **the chair**. After finishing his intense work with the student, he turned around to head back for his chair. Without changing his expression, or his stride, he calmly sat on the couch next to **the chair**. He then completely relaxed on the couch where the students usually sit. Turning my test around into a wonderful joke, he made me sit in his chair for the rest of the lesson. I found it very hard to relax in **the chair** and squirmed quite a bit during those few minutes.

It seems nearly impossible to take Suzuki by surprise. In all the time I have been here I have seen it happen only once. When a student makes some awful noise on an exercise that Suzuki makes seem so simple, Suzuki always asks, "Do you like noise?" Of course, for years everyone has always said, "No!" But one day, in a circumstance in which we could all foresee the coming dialogue, the student replied, "Yes!" Dr. Suzuki was just beginning his next sentence when he stopped, looked at the student, and had the most incredible look of surprise on his face. Then he started laughing and laughing. Just when we thought he had recovered, he went over to his chair, and starting laughing again until tears rolled down his cheeks. Finally he stopped, became very serious, and said, "That has never happened before.'' Of course, that started a new round of laughter.

Being around Suzuki makes me feel that I want to give him something or do something for him. His spirit is so giving that it just spreads easily to many people. Of course, not everyone catches that spirit and the giving of Suzuki. I cannot understand how that can be, but it does happen sometimes.

Anyway, most people feel like they want to give Suzuki something. I have seen him receive some fantastic gifts and react with pure and simple joy. I feel sure that he would react just as fully and completely if someone were to give him a marshmallow (though he does like chocolates best.) Once, when he wasn't looking, I put a piece of his favorite chocolate by his seat in the auditorium. When he returned to his seat, his whole face lit up, and he started to chuckle. He looked all around the auditorium to see if he could tell who did it. Finally, he broke off little pieces and gave everyone around him some of his chocolate. When there was only a little piece left, he sat down again, looked at the chocolate, chuckled and waited. Then he put it into his mouth and started to chuckle all over again.

His responses are always 100 per cent, and there is no pretense of joy. There is just joy. To me, it seems that Suzuki has everything he needs to be happy — he is just happy. So it makes me feel like I want to give something and do something for another person. I wonder if that is part of the ''Suzuki Method?''

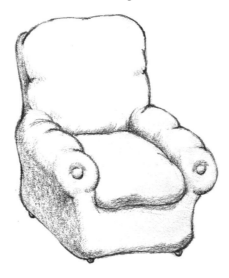

When Is Suzuki?

Gosh, what a funny question. It is one that I wouldn't have asked a while ago. It doesn't seem to make sense. But the more I watch Suzuki, the more things change in my mind. Actually, I think this is a very important question and is closely related to the question, "Where Is Suzuki?"

The answer to "When is Suzuki?" is, of course, "Now". Suzuki is always now. That is why he is alway here. I think that this may be one of the reasons that it is so very special to be in the presence of Suzuki. When he gives you his attention he gives 100 per cent, and the results are incredible.

When he is giving a lesson he isn't thinking about what he is going to have for supper. I am quite confident that even when he gives a lesson just before an important meeting he is still within the "now" of the lesson. Perhaps that is why he can react so fully to things that happen around him.

The proof of these ideas came one day not long ago, when someone asked him what he was going to do tomorrow. He got a very puzzled look on his face, and had to go into his office and check his schedule. "Oh yes," he replied, "Tomorrow I go to Tokyo!"

When an idea such as this strikes me I like to experiment with it. I have found that I can enjoy the most amazing things in this fashion — things like the ticking of a clock, walking long distances, even washing dishes. For some reason I have not been able to enjoy straightening up my room, but that might come some day too. It does seem a bit far-fetched, but one never knows.

My Discovery

When I was in kindergarten, a violinist came to our class. He was an entertainer of sorts, and while he played I decided that I too wanted to play the violin. For weeks I asked my parents every day if I could play the violin. They were wise, thinking that this phase would pass if they let me keep asking. Anyway, I remember thinking for many nights that if I prayed hard enough, maybe, when I woke up, there would be a violin beside my bed. Finally one day my mother said, "Today we are going to get your violin." I can vividly remember getting into the car, going to a room full of violins, and finding one the right size for me. I was overjoyed to finally have gotten a violin. I think it is good that I can't remember the first sounds I made on my violin.

The sad part of this tale is that the day I got my violin was four years after the day I decided that that was what I wanted. In those days there was no way for a very young child to start the violin — there was no Suzuki method then.

At first my enthusiasm made me learn very quickly, and I even wanted to practice. I found it a joy and privilege to be playing my violin. My parents and teacher were excited by my progress, and began to encourage me. Soon I moved to the front of the class of little violinists. Then the trouble started. It was thought that perhaps I could "amount to something" if I really practiced. So I was "encouraged" to practice even harder. But somehow all of this encouragement to practice more made my enthusiasm start to fade. I can remember the days very clearly when I would close the door to my room, practice a little bit, then open my window, jump out, and go play with my friends. As I got older I grew a bit more sophisticated in avoiding practice. In those days tape recorders were beginning to be available, and I got one when I was in Junior High School. I would record half of my allotted practice time, then play back the tape while I read a book in the same room. I don't think my parents knew my secret until they read the draft of this paper.

This situation continued, and in this sad state I eventually went to college to learn to become a violin teacher. At first the newness of college made me want to practice. But then one day a teacher came to me and said, "I don't waste my time on people who don't practice. If you want lessons from me you are going to really have to work. Don't you dare try to waste my time!"

Of course, none of these people was wrong. But there was something in me that faded under such pressure. What had once been a joy became a chore that I did only out of guilt. I always practiced because I felt I "must," never because I felt like I wanted to. Even when I started teaching I felt like this.

Eventually, I even came to Japan with the same attitude. In a way, I felt it was wrong to come to Japan because my rebellion towards practice was very deep and very strong. Luckily I came anyway.

There is a teacher here who believes that the most important thing about learning is first to create desire. But it took even Suzuki six months to rekindle my desire to practice. I had almost twenty years of forced practice and negative memories to erase. Suzuki had the patience to allow every one of those years to drop out of my mind. What a shattering my resistance went through. Now I can hardly wait to get up in the morning, or to get home from a class, so that I can practice. I can pay no greater tribute to Suzuki than to say that he created a strong desire in me to practice.

Tonight I began my practice in a normal way, with tonalization, when suddenly an urge hit me to study an idea about the bow. Within a few minutes, I began to realize something very special about the use of the bow, and got very excited. I kept playing, practicing tonalization and getting more and more interested and excited about what I was doing and what I had discovered. I could hardly wait to see Dr. Suzuki and tell him of my discovery when, suddenly, I started laughing — laughing with excitement, joy, and admiration for Suzuki. I hadn't discovered anything at all! I had only been following the subtle clues that Suzuki had been putting in front of me. As I began to get closer and closer to the final clue, I got more excited and studied harder without realizing why. When I finally made my "discovery", I realized that Suzuki had been giving me clues for six months! It just had taken me that long to follow them up.

I came to Japan holding Suzuki in the highest esteem as a teacher and person. But I am beginning to realize that I have been underestimating him. Not only am I just beginning to realize what a teacher he really is, but I am also beginning to realize that I can't understand completely what kind of teacher he is. There is so much depth that I just can't see past the beginning. In thirty minutes Suzuki could have explained completely in theory what had taken me months to "discover". But perhaps he knew how I would react to a theory, so he remained patient with me until I "discovered" and got enjoyment out of studying the problem for myself.

If anyone tells me, "Do it this way," or "You must do so and so," I always react strongly against those forced conditions. Suzuki, sensing this, taught me how it feels to "discover." In a way he really wasn't trying to teach me about the bow at all. All this time, I had been watching, listening, trying to pick up all the subtleties that he was throwing out, studying, learning, and finding clues. Perhaps he was trying to show me something about motivation and teaching. Now, I suppose I'll have to start catching his clues to see if I can find the answer.

Don't Talk

The Japanese teachers have a joke about American teachers. They say, "In Japan we teach for 27 minutes and talk for three; in America they talk for 27 minutes and teach for three." Gosh, did I laugh when I heard that one. To me it was another "cosmic joke." But ultimately it struck deep down and revealed a secret to me.

I was fortunate enough to have read Timothy Gallwey's book, *Inner Tennis*, before I studied with Suzuki. It put me in the frame of mind to let my inner self do the learning. However, it wasn't until I heard this "joke" that I was struck with what "Don't Talk" really means.

I remember how much fun we foreign students had watching a "new foreigner's" lesson. We always made sure not to miss these occasions — to support the new person, to learn, but also to savor the enjoyment we got from it.

Invariably, Suzuki would say something, and the student, with his Western training, would ask a question. We were always delighted at the astonished look on Suzuki's face when a student asked a question.

One of Suzuki's arts is question answering. Whenever he answers a question, it seems like he has actually answered the question. Later, one finds that he has actually only made the issue more cloudy. At the time, however, new students usually look like they understand the answer, and then blithely proceed with the lesson. It almost seems like Suzuki confuses the rational mind so much that the "inner mind" has to take over.

I often puzzled over this strange behavior. Lately, however, I have begun to realize that teaching to the inner person is really a short cut. For any theory to be of use to us on the instrument, we must practice the theory so diligently that it seeps into the unconscious mind. The Japanese call this "the underground sense." I think this is where the "10,000 times" exercise comes in. During that exercise, there is a connection to the "underground." Then the next exercise gets "through" much faster and the "inner self" learns more quickly.

Gradually, it seemed that instead of teaching the rational person, and then letting it seep into the underground, Suzuki would begin to teach the underground sense directly. At these times, the words he used were complete nonsense to us, and our rational minds started going in circles. Then he was able to demonstrate directly to the "underground sense."

In some strange way, the idea of "Don't Talk" began to be an attitude or state of mind, where the judgmental part of the brain left us alone so that the other parts of us could learn some new ability more quickly and easily. In this state, the rational mind is the last part of us to learn and acknowledge a new skill or ability. The first time I did the 10,000 times exercise, I felt that a light went on in my head.

In the beginning, I thought that the talking Suzuki did sounded funny because English was a foreign language to him. But as I worked with the Japanese people around him, I found out that he was able to confuse people in just about any language, until they were ready to let go and start learning the easy way.

It seems that after months in the atmosphere of "Don't Talk," my mind became quiet. Not only did my mouth not talk, but all of the internal noises began to fade too, and my ability to concentrate with my whole mind grew. In this atmosphere, the talking part of my brain began to grow quiet and calm, and I was prepared to learn.

Often nowadays, when someone asks me about some point that I must have learned from Suzuki, I get all tongue-tied. I find that my underground knows the answer, but the reasoning part of my brain doesn't. It seems that, after months with Suzuki, one just naturally falls into the habit of watching for answers. It begins to be a way of living, I suppose.

I wonder if this all relates to the maxim, "Silence is the beginning of wisdom."

Nothing

> *One of the most significant features we notice in the practice of archery, and in fact of all the arts as they are studied in Japan . . . is that they are not intended for utilitarian purposes only or for purely aesthetic enjoyments, but are meant to train the mind; indeed, to bring it into contact with the ultimate reality . . . The mind first has to be attuned to the Unconscious.* [1]

After I had been in Japan for some time, Suzuki began to do something that made me feel very strange. After every group lesson he would come to me and ask, "What did you think about group lesson today?" He always caught me off guard, because I was trying to not think or judge the group lesson, the teacher or myself, or my reactions, but only to be as aware as possible of the teacher and myself. But whenever Suzuki asked me this question I felt I had to say something, so I would quickly make up some kind of answer. He would smile, even chuckle, then say something in response, and be off. After this was repeated for some weeks I began to dread the end of the group lesson, for he would find me and ask me this question every time, and I always felt very uncomfortable when he did so. Finally I could bear it no longer, and when he asked me again, "What did you think about group lesson today?" I answered, "Nothing!" He looked at me with curiosity, gave me a wonderful sparkle with his eyes and chuckled. Then he said, "Ah so," gave me a deep bow, and never asked me that question again.

As students at the Suzuki School we also studied calligraphy with a "master." I enjoyed it immensely for a number of weeks before I began to notice something strange. *Sensei* would make corrections in our efforts, and I watched her very closely as she corrected several students on the same character. But she would tell each person something a bit different. I began to suspect that there was something more to this business than what was appearing on the surface. It was almost as if *Sensei* wasn't correcting the art work itself, or asking us to change the art, but that she wanted us to change something about ourselves.

When I compared what she was doing to what Suzuki was doing on the violin I got some interesting insights. Often Suzuki would ask different students to play the same piece in specific but different ways. I began to feel that he wasn't talking about how to actually do the art itself, but was really asking the question, "Where is your art coming from?" We were really being taught to let our art become so completely natural that we wouldn't need to think about it at all. Instead we could loosen our minds and let the music flow through us.

Perhaps this is why Suzuki wants students to repeat pieces so often that they can play them and talk at the same time. When this happens, the music begins to come not from our thinking, but to flow through us. Perhaps this is why the children play with the accompaniment tape over 300 times each year until they graduate from "Book Ten." I think that this is all connected to Suzuki saying "10,000 times," and the strange thing that happened to me when I actually did an exercise that many times.

> *The archer ceases to be conscious of himself as the one who is engaged in hitting the bull's-eye which confronts him. This state of unconsciousness is realized only when, completely empty and rid of the self, he becomes one with the perfecting of his technical skill, though there is in it something of a quite different order which cannot be attained by any progressive study of the art.*[2]

------

1. *Zen in the Art of Archery* by Eugen Herrigel, copyright 1953 Pantheon Books, a division of Random House, Inc., New York.
2. *ibid.*

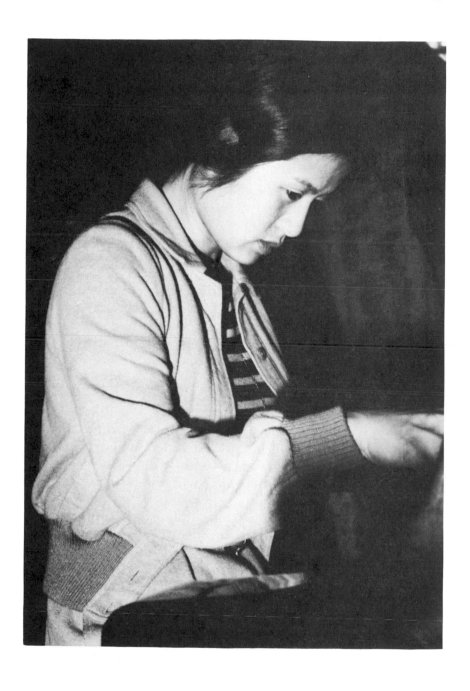

Please Don't Review

Can you believe that I would actually say, "Don't review?" It seems to go against the Suzuki Method. "My goodness," you might say, "if we don't review, how can we play in group lessons or other events?"

I think that our concepts of "review" and the reasons we review are not exactly what Suzuki has in mind. It doesn't seem to be thought of in the same way in Japan as it is in America. I will be the first to say that I always wanted my students to review even before I went to Japan, but only to the extent that they could play every piece that they had learned with proper fingers and bow. The longer I taught, the more important I thought review was. However, now I don't believe in review. I hope that I never use the word or let students or parents think in those terms.

Often I am astonished in group lessons or workshops when children can only fumble through pieces. They seem to be able to play only the piece they are presently polishing. These children quickly lose their desire and motivation even to come to group. Their overall confidence on their instrument begins to drop off, and many times they misbehave in class so that no one can notice that they cannot play.

I never saw this happen in Japan. There could be many reasons for this, but I think one of them is that the Japanese don't review. That is why the children in any group lesson or large gathering can always play every piece with the correct fingerings, bowings, and even musicality. I remember that Suzuki said, "Ability is developed when we study a piece after we can play it with no mistakes." It is at this point we can work on **music**. This is the time when the child begins to play naturally and without effort. This is when confidence develops. The willingness to work on something after this stage helps the student grow in other areas of living. It is for this reason that Suzuki always said, "Play some nice piece." It was our job to learn the piece. Then Suzuki would help in an area of technical difficulty, but mostly he would help us develop musicality and naturalness in our playing.

For this reason the Japanese teachers ask their students to

play the pieces hundreds of times during the year — not for review, but **to develop ability!** By repeated study, striving to make something better, the students are then able to learn new pieces and techniques faster. The repetitions do not slow progress; they actually speed progress as they develop ability.

Decrescendo

To a musician, this mark $\rightharpoondown$ means *decrescendo*. To me it also means an idea that is similar, but refers to a thought process instead of a musical idea. It reminds me of the method of teaching that I saw and experienced in Japan.

In the West, when we want someone to notice something, we tell them in the biggest possible way. This is true of talking, teaching, advertising or anything else. The more important we think the idea is, the larger we make the presentation.

When I first started watching children's lessons in Japan, I was watching with my Western kind of background. I was constantly amazed that the children could learn anything, because it looked like the teacher wasn't presenting anything to them at all. I couldn't understand how the children could play so well when there didn't seem to be anything going on, or so little of something that I couldn't catch the drift of it. As it turned out, perhaps that is why they could play so well; it might just be the key to their astuteness.

At first, in my lessons with Suzuki I was confused. I had thought that he always taught a one point lesson, but my lessons seemed to have many points. After some weeks of study, however, I found to my surprise that my lessons did indeed have only one point, but I had failed to catch what the point really was. From then on I studied my lesson tape much more carefully, to observe how Suzuki approached the same point from so many different angles. Gradually I began to catch the point easier and faster, and my lessons got shorter. As soon as Suzuki knew that I had found the point, tonalization was finished. After he helped me apply the same point to my piece for the day, the lesson was over. I began to see that my progress increased even though my lessons grew shorter.

I saw that Suzuki and all the teachers I observed started out as diffuse as the students. Gradually, however, after many one point lessons, the student's concentration became so finely tuned that the slightest indication by the teacher on a point would be enough for the student to catch and pick up on. By "getting smaller" the teachers helped the students' awareness grow so intense that they could concentrate beautifully, and the speed of learning was multiplied. When this happens the relationship between the teacher and student is something that almost defies description. I offer that observation from watching the relationship of the teachers and students in Japan, and from my own experience with my lessons there. This heightened awareness is carried around with the student in every aspect of life in learning and in human relations. Eventually we can see it in the face of a musician who is so completely immersed in the music that he becomes the music.

"When I Am 90 I Will Be A Teacher"

I vividly remember a group lesson in Japan when Suzuki was explaining a new point and there were many confused-looking faces among the student teachers. As he noticed those looks, he started to tell a story—first in Japanese, then in English.

When Suzuki was in Germany he knew some students who were studying with a renowned teacher. But the students were very disgruntled. They said to Suzuki, "One week he says, 'This is the way you must play the violin.' We practice very hard to play this way, and then at the next lesson he says, 'It is impossible to play the violin like that; you must play like this.' Every week he changes and says to play a different way." So Dr. Suzuki went to this teacher and asked him if this could possibly be true. He replied, "Of course it is true. In one week I learn so many new things that I find out what I knew last week couldn't possibly be true."

Although Suzuki never gave what could be described as a

definitive answer to the only way of playing, he was always
learning new points about how to play, how to teach, and how to
help people.

For months I heard Suzuki say, "For student—easy, for
teacher—very difficult." All of us student teachers thought it was
a good joke. Even though the children could play things we
couldn't, and do memory feats that we couldn't, it still somehow
seemed like a joke. Some of us began to get suspicious though
when he once said, "For teacher this is impossible; for student it
is easy."

I began to think that he felt we should continue to be
students so we could learn how to play the violin and make
music. But one day, Suzuki smacked me with his "hammer". He
told me, "I will be a student until I am 90 years old; then I will be
a teacher." He has only a few more years of studenthood to go!

As I look around me now, and look over the past years I can
see that the people who were working on themselves were the
people that helped me too. They felt that they didn't have the
answers, but were just beginning to understand. They didn't try
to force answers into me, but, because of their searching, they
inspired me to look also.

It seems that once we start to search, we begin to know how
to search. The journey for truth and knowledge seems to push us
along its own course, and the less we fight it the faster we move.

Years ago, I had several aquariums and I remember putting
new fish into the tank. If the fish were weak in any way, the other
fish would pick on their weakness. I think that is very much like
nature and our search as students. We don't seem to have to
worry about what to work on in our lives—nature always seems
to aim at the weakest point in us, then we see what to work on
and how. If we don't work on it, nature will keep picking at that
place until something gives way.

I can remember in my childhood studying about how
lightning strikes. It always takes the path of least resistance, to
the weakest point, so to speak. I can remember wondering how
the lightning floating around in the clouds could figure out
which point was the weakest, and then strike there. Actually, I
still wonder about that sometimes. However, the lightning never
wonders; it has kept on striking the weakest point all the years I

haven't been able to figure it out.

Sometimes I think I am beginning to understand what Dr. Suzuki meant when he said, "Difficult for teacher; easy for student." When I feel like a "teacher" I must assume that I know the answer to something or other. This place always seems to turn out to be the weakest point, because that is where the lightning strikes.

Another Letter From Japan To My Students

In this installment I have some exciting episodes to relate. Soon after I finish writing this I will leave for Tokyo for the big all-Japan annual concert. This year will be a bit extraordinary because it will also be the celebration of the Suzukis' 50th wedding anniversary.

Yesterday, in preparation, I went to the Hair Saron. Yes, the spelling is correct. Of course, we usually say "Hair Salon". but there is some difficulty here with the understanding and pronunciation of "L" and "R". Anyway, it is always a real treat to go to a barber in Japan. The one I go to so enjoys cutting foreigners' hair that he does all kinds of wonderful extra things.

I have great fun just letting things happen here, since there is no way for me to control anything anyway. Today my "haircut" took one hour and 45 minutes. First I got a shampoo, then a razor cut, then a wonderful head, neck and back massage. When this barber works it is very much like a ballet. The grace and style that the man used today were a joy to watch. After the first hour of enjoyment, the barber got out a beautiful razor. He was going to give me a shave, I supposed. With great relish and flurry, he covered me in hot steaming towels. Then he mixed soap in a mug, sharpened his wonderful razor, and gave me a delightful shave.

Suddenly, however, he took hold of my ear, pulled it out, and started coming toward it with the razor. I tell you, my heart missed several beats, and sweat popped out very suddenly. I knew my ears had always stuck out a bit, but I thought there was really no need to cut them off!!

Amazingly, what he did was to shave my ears! I don't mean behind my ears, or around my ears, I mean that he shaved my ears. Then he shaved my forehead, then he shaved my neck. During this time I didn't move a muscle I assure you. Even if I could have spoken Japanese to the man, my mouth wouldn't have worked had I tried.

When he finished, I am afraid I let out an audible sigh and leaned back with relief that I was still all there. The barber, to make sure that I got completely relaxed after my ordeal, spread some kind of hot, green mud all over my face. Then he eventually removed it with a pile of steaming towels and finished things off with another massage. All this came when I only asked for a "Haircut." Indeed this was the only word I spoke the whole time. I must say that that is what I call a real haircut! I hope my barber in Mankato reads this, because I want him to know what I expect when I return.

Also quite fresh in my memory is my recent meal in a *Sushi* restaurant. *Sushi* is a hand-formed ball of rice with something placed on or in it. Usually the something is some kind of raw seafood.

One of my teachers here took me to the restaurant for a special supper. He asked me what kind of *Sushi* I like, and I said, "Anything except raw squid." We went into this very classical restaurant and sat at the counter, which was made of marble. Behind the counter was a beautiful display of raw clams and oysters, fish and various other seafoods. At the front of our counter little streams of water squirted into a trough so that we could rinse our hands as often as we liked.

My teacher ordered three meals of *Sushi* and left to the *chefs* what they would serve us. They quickly produced the best *Sushi* that I have ever tasted. The food was remarkably fresh. The clams, shrimps, etc. were on ice, and the *chef* took them from their shells and prepared them before our eyes. I had raw clams, raw oysters, raw shrimp and some other things that I couldn't identify. Then came some kind of fish eggs. They were almost identical to vitamin E pills in size, shape, color, and even taste. I had some trouble getting that rice ball down. Though I did succeed, I left the second one uneaten. My teacher watched me discreetly with a twinkle in his eye.

Then came the raw squid! There was no way out of eating this one since the *chef* had prepared it especially for me, and I was a guest. So after a certain amount of procrastination, during which the teacher was having a marvelous time, I began to eat the squid. This teacher was very much like Suzuki in many ways, and I wanted to trust him as well as please him. I must admit that the squid was quite edible, and nothing like my first experience with the dish. I later found out that my first taste of squid was definitely not fresh enough. I cannot say that it was delicious or that I would order it again, but I can say that I am glad I trusted my teacher. Of course we all had a good laugh after I had finished my squid, and the *Sensei* said to me, "Probably today your stomach is astonished." I laughed so hard at this that it was all I could do to remain on my stool.

Perhaps to settle my astonished stomach, after our main course we proceeded to a coffee restaurant. The restaurant was decorated with good taste and reserve. It was full of beautifully restored antiques. The coffee was delicious and did indeed settle my stomach. It wasn't until later that I found out that those small cups of coffee we had enjoyed so much cost $3.00 per cup!

More Of Suzuki

For many years I thought that Suzuki was giving a message to the West by writing only one book, somehow saying everything that he wanted to say in that compact way. Wise, perhaps, but I rather wished there was more of it for us. Imagine my surprise upon arriving in Japan to find that Suzuki has written many books and scores of magazine articles. I was not only surprised, but aghast that none of these books had been translated.

After a while I was approached by the Japanese man who taught English to the Suzuki kindergarten. "Let us translate some of Dr. Suzuki's work into English," he said. Since I could only speak four words of Japanese, I didn't see how I could do any translating, and Mr. Nakagaki told me that my work would be quite difficult. In retrospect I can say that the labor I spent on small bits of Suzuki's work was indeed strenuous and mind wrenching.

I can begin to understand the enormous task that Mrs. Suzuki undertook when she translated *Nurtured by Love*. She had to look up almost every word in a dictionary. Japanese characters have many meanings, so she had to choose the correct ones. Once the words were translated into English they made very little sense at all. Concepts well known in the East mean nothing to us, so a good portion of the text was only mishmash. Somehow the thoughts had to be translated into English concepts, and yet the spirit of Suzuki kept alive. The simple clarity must not be destroyed, yet the ambiguities must not be clarified for they provoke deep thinking. So my part in the translation was to try to make sense out of the English that didn't make sense. Our teamwork did not dent the piles of paper to be translated, and could hardly be considered anything more than a taste. But gradually now, things are being translated into English for us. The following article is quite a meaningful example:

———

"The Ability To Feel Another Person's Heart"
by Shinichi Suzuki[1]

I am pondering the statement, "Art is the Man." In music, sound has life without shape or form, but it lives. In the best Beethoven, Bach or Mozart, the composers' high and beautiful minds, their viewpoint of life, and character are revealed very clearly. Their compositions transfer these feelings to our minds.

How deeply we can absorb or appreciate the composer's "voice of life" as listeners depends on our level of growth as human beings. Some people feel one thing, and other people feel something else; it depends on the level of sensitivity in the listener.

If we repeatedly train our ability and communicate with each other "spirit to spirit", then as listeners we develop the ability to appreciate art on higher levels, and the listener himself will be changed gradually and grow in humanity.

At first we might just be enchanted by the music, whether we understand it or not. But as we just listen to the music repeatedly we will be led into the world of beauty. As we listen to the music over and over again the music talks to us and tells us about the composer's heart. Gradually we will be able to feel the "voice of life."

Every time we hear a repetition we gain more of the ability "to feel another's heart;" gradually we will be able to understand the composer's heart. As we keep on communicating with each other "spirit to spirit" we will be able to understand that "Art is the Man."

Education in its highest level will lead children to become very fine people with beautiful minds and high hearts. Our purpose in music education is to help our students to recognize beauty, nobility and high humanity that composers such as Bach, Mozart, and Beethoven had. However, we can only appreciate the spirit of another person to the level of our own development. Dogs and cats can hear our sounds but they are not developed enough to be able to understand our talking. Cows will give more milk if we play music during their milking; perhaps this is because the music is pleasant. But as humans, we are different; we are able to feel the touching together of spirits — heart to heart. We can create a very high level world in which we communicate to each other with high spirits like Mozart or Beethoven.

It is our greatest privilege as human beings, that we have "hearts" and can see the beautiful and high world of life.

Of course we can develop our ability to feel another person's heart in other areas besides music — for instance, in the education of etiquette or courtesy. It is more important to arrange our hearts than it is to change our outside shape or form. Once we feel another person's heart, we respect them and never want to hurt them. We would be able to never speak against this person. Then we would understand respect for another person. I think that there is no difference between music and this kind of etiquette.

In *Nurtured by Love* I wrote about an incident with Koji Toyoda. Koji asked Professor Enesco if he could be allowed to become his student. The professor replied, "You are now studying with Professor Benedetti at the Paris Conservatory; I could not be so discourteous to him and accept you as a student. When you have graduated from the Paris Conservatory please come to see me."

This is indeed proof that Professor Enesco was a wonderful teacher with a high heart and excellent art. We can see his greatness in his courtesy.

It is very regretful that people in Japan do not act with this courtesy. People neglect the substance of art. I am pondering — "Art is the Man." I had a fine student that I had been teaching for a long time, and I thought I would have him go abroad to study with a great maestro. But suddenly he was studying with a teacher in Tokyo. Only after the student moved did the father write to me and thank me for taking care of his son through all the years. This made me feel very sad and lonely.

Of course the student didn't move to another teacher by himself — he moved because of his parents' will. Had the parents only asked me to move to another teacher I would have written an introduction letter and asked the new teacher to take care of the student. However, the parents didn't say a word before they moved; they wrote only after they had already moved.

They didn't understand what I feel in my heart towards my students. They didn't know that I had loved the student just like my own child for ten years and they cut the string between us without saying anything beforehand.

I plead with all parents in the Talent Education Program: please do not do such a thing to your teacher. If we nurture a student for five or ten years we are tied together with a string from heart to heart. If you want to move to another teacher, talk to your present teacher first without hesitation. This is the kind of etiquette and respect that we should use.

If the parents want to move to another teacher, of course the teachers in our Institute will write to the new teacher and ask that he take care of our former student along with a letter of introduction.

Last year I had five students move away without warning. This made me feel very sad. Art does not stand without etiquette. Please understand that the students and teachers are in one family. We should use respect for each other to get along with each other in a polite and happy life.

Professor Enesco is a very good person; he had a beautiful heart and a very high spirit in humanity. This is "Art."

The parents who severed their child's relationship with me made me feel betrayed. That is why I ponder the statement so seriously, "Art is the Man."

––––––

1. *Talent Education Magazine*, Winter 1977 No. 39. Translated by Toshihiko Nakagaki and Craig Timmerman, Matsumoto, Japan March 1977. Used by permission.

A Multiplier Of Effectiveness

We have all heard how Oriental people respect their teachers. The very word "teacher" in Japanese is one of the words of highest respect in the language. When I went to Japan, I took with me my American perception of teachers, that is to regard everything the teacher says with healthy skepticism and make him prove everything, or at least check it out first to be certain that it is correct.

With my American attitude, I was amused when I observed just how highly the Japanese respect their teachers. In the beginning I actually made light of this aspect of Japan. Of course I respected Suzuki greatly, but not in the same way that the Japanese did.

My first inkling of doubt came one day when I was in the communal practice room. I looked around to see what the 20 or so people were practicing on, and I noticed one Japanese student-teacher making small circles with her bow in front of a mirror. This was an exercise I saw Suzuki assign many students, so I was already familiar with it. When he assigns it he always says, "10,000 times." The Americans usually laugh, and go on to something different.

Anyway, I turned to the wall and began my practice. When I turned around 30 minutes later, the Japanese girl was again making circles in front of the looking glass. Of course, I knew that it was just a coincidence that she was doing the same thing I had observed 30 minutes previously. I knew that she just did that intermittently, but observing as I did, it almost looked like she had done it for 30 minutes straight. I smiled and went back to work.

The next day, I came in to practice about the same time, and there was the same girl in front of the mirror again. This time, just to prove to myself that my previous day's observation was an illusion, I found a spot where I could face the girl while I practiced without being noticed. She did the exercise for a full 30 minutes before going on to something else! I shook my head, packed up my instrument and went for a walk, mumbling to myself as I did so.

When the same thing happened the third day, it was just too much for me. I approached the girl and said to her, "What are you doing?" She replied, "*Sensei* told me to do this 10,000 times. That means 30 minutes per day for two weeks." I said, "But that is only a joke!" "Oh, is it?" she replied, and continued.

I thought to myself, "Of course, she is Japanese and probably didn't understand Suzuki's sense of humor." All of the foreign students laughed when Suzuki said "10,000 times" and felt they were getting his humor. I did the exercise a few times during the week and would make a larger effort just before my lesson, but I knew all the time that he didn't really mean 10,000 times, not really.

After this episode though, I decided to try it once for myself and see if it really was a joke. Luckily my assignment was very small, so I really could easily do it 5,000 times per week. Somewhere around the end of the first week, my mouth fell open. After so many repetitions something inside me sparked, and the exercise became increasingly more meaningful and exciting. By the time I had reached 10,000 I had a deeper understanding of why the Japanese respect their teachers and each word they say.

From that point on, Suzuki would give me an exercise and say, with a sparkle in his eyes, "Perhaps 2,000 is enough now." Needless to say, I was happy about the lower number, but I was always curious to know how Suzuki could tell I had actually done one lesson 10,000 times.

I began to study the parents and children taking lessons from various teachers at the Institute. There was such a great unquestioning respect for the teacher, and there was a freedom and a speed of learning going on that was hard to believe. The teacher never had to wheedle or coax a child to do an exercise; it was just accepted and worked on. Soon I began to notice that this respect carried over into many other areas. The students' attention was very acute and tuned to the teacher so that they could catch what the teacher wanted. Not only did this make it immensely easier to teach but, unbeknown to the child, it also greatly increased his own awareness and powers of observation.

I recall what a good friend of mine in America, a very fine teacher, once said. She tells her students when they go away to college, "You will be going to a different teacher with many ideas that might seem to conflict with mine. When you study with this teacher you should trust him to be infallible. If you have doubts or force him to coax you along, you will be wasting his time and yours. To take full benefit of your teacher, whoever he may be, you should trust and respect him completely while you study with him. Later you will have the opportunity to look at other angles on your own, but if you truly want to learn from this teacher you must follow him 100 per cent."

She had never been to Japan, but she had certainly summed up the essence of the learning attitude. I suspect that it was not a coincidence that her students were such respectful, kind and quick people — just the sort one enjoys being around.

No! You Must Do It This Way!

Who is right? What an important question to think about. It is especially timely when workshop season is upon us. One of the best things about the national and international propagation of Suzuki's teachings through workshops is that we begin to leave behind us many regional ideas and begin to get a much broader perspective on music, playing, and living. This is important for us personally, and it is essential that people of the world begin to understand each other.

I think that any time there is a small pocket of people in a closed environment, it is easy for those people to feel that the way they do things is the only right way, or at least the best way. Then they become unable to learn from people from other places with differing ideas. It certainly doesn't help education. Nor does it lead to making the "small earth" that Suzuki talks of so often.

I hope that in my teaching I don't give the impression that a certain way is the only correct way to play, to make music, or to solve a certain problem. I have no set answers to every problem or situation.

My biggest hope for my students is to help prepare them to learn, to be flexible, to be ready and able to learn quickly — not only from me, but from any source.

These students can then learn from so many of life's valuable resources — records, parents, other performances, other teachers, things like trees, flowers and birds. These students can become students of life and can bring this education to their music. Not only will they be able to learn quickly, but they will also have something very special in their music.

I think Suzuki taught us teacher trainees in this way. Sometimes we would study some point very diligently and he would say, "Yes but now I have a better idea than the one from last week." My first reaction to this was, "Gosh, all that time wasted and all that work for nothing." Gradually though, I found that I was becoming more flexible in my thinking, which helped me to learn faster from Suzuki and from life. I am not sure Suzuki did that on purpose; I hardly think so. Yet great advantages came from that situation.

The famous concert violist, William Primrose, who came to teach in Matsumoto several times a year, said to us many times, "If it works for you, it is the right way; there isn't an **only correct way**." Suzuki seemed to say the same thing in his actions and teaching.

If we can teach our students in this way the question of "Who is right — this teacher or that teacher?" need never be asked. In fact, both are right, even if they say opposite things. The real question is, "Are we flexible enough to be able to learn from whomever or whatever is our teacher of the moment?"

But I Thought That Was The Way Everyone Does It

Some of the most valuable education I have received while living in Japan has little to do with the violin, yet it has everything to do with people. I am convinced that Suzuki observed the same thing when he lived in Germany, and that his observations led eventually to the discovery of "mother tongue" learning. Each day in this foreign country, I realize more and more the completeness of the education of the total being that comes from the environment. It is almost frightening to realize that even the way we think is trained into us.

My first big lesson came when I ate dinner in a nice Western style restaurant with a Japanese, an Australian, a Frenchman and some Americans. It turned out that the Japanese man had not eaten with silverware before, so he asked us some simple questions, like how to cut his meat. **We all had different answers!**

Do you know that we are consciously trained in how to use our silverware? We Americans put the knife in our dominant hand and cut, then put down the knife and pick up the fork in the dominant hand, one bite at a time. That is the only polite way to do it in America, at least to my knowledge. I don't remember being trained in this at all, and to this day I wouldn't know I was trained in it except for the fact that the Europeans had a very definite answer that was different from mine. The Europeans, of course, put the knife in the non-dominant hand

and do not switch back and forth. The Australian said, "You must hold your knife in your hand until all the meat is cut." Who could imagine that we are trained to eat? I thought there was just a "natural" way that everyone used. The poor Japanese man had a very difficult time, but he eventually got his meal from his plate to his mouth. I don't remember whose method he used.

In studying the American language I find that we are trained in some of the most subtle ways. Different parts of our country speak with different and quite definite speeds, let alone dialects. We train our tongues to make certain kinds of sounds. By the time we are adults, that training has become so ingrained that it is virtually impossible to train our tongues to accurately make the sounds of another language.

In America the aim seems to be to train everyone to be leaders, public speakers, independent thinkers and individualists. In Japan people are trained to be group conscious; they are trained to sacrifice immensely for the group, their company, etc.

It is immediately apparent, even to me, when a Japanese person has studied abroad and brought back with him attitudes different from the "Japanese way." Actually, it is an unspoken rule that if a Japanese stays out of Japan for more that four years at a time, it will be almost impossible for him to find a job when he returns. Employers are very leery because the person has lost too much of the Japanese way.

The point of these observations is not to say who is right or wrong, but to be shocked into the realization that we are trained in every way by our environment, in ways so minute and subtle that they are virtually impossible to detect. Living in a foreign place brings these minute differences out in startling discoveries. I begin to see ever more clearly why Suzuki works so determinedly to help create better environments for all children everywhere. The real proportions of his work are just beginning to dawn on me.

I hope that among the other qualities in the environment we can create around our children, we can train them to be open and accepting of other people's ways. Thus, they can avoid the trap of feeling that their way is the only right way and any different way is wrong.

Gee! That Was Just For Me

Recently I was sitting in a room full of Japanese people, friendly and kind enough, but engaged in conversation with each other in Japanese. I couldn't understand anything, and even their body language was beyond my comprehension. However, I was not able to leave the room for a long time so I had to sit. As my mind began to wander and I grew bored, I began cooking up some mischief that would at least get some reactions that I could understand. Even if they weren't reactions of pure joy, I didn't care. I only needed something I could understand.

Just when I had formulated my plan and was about to set it into action, someone spoke to me in English and offered me a piece of candy. Wow! Just ten seconds of kind attention, and I glowed the rest of the time I was in the room. I even stayed interested in things I couldn't understand.

Now I think I can understand why little children react so beautifully to a pat on the back, a squeeze of the hand, or a smile. Their whole lives are spent in an environment that they cannot comprehend. Everything is over their heads. They are full of such wonderful energy, but are asked to contain it and pay attention to something they can't understand. I suppose it bothers me more than the children because I know another way. I am accustomed to being in situations where I can understand things, where I can understand every word that is spoken and not have to strain, where I can respond without being told that my response was improper or impolite. The child has an advantage here, I guess, for he doesn't know that there is this other way to live. He just has to sit and "pay attention."

It seems to me just a little smile or hug once in a while can bring sunshine into a child's life. It might be one of the only things that happens in a whole day that the child can really understand.

An Article Of Interest

Today I saw a Japanese mother and child hugging and laughing for joy after a lesson. At first I couldn't imagine this going on at lesson time, but then it dawned on me that they were both thrilled to the point of hugging because of their lesson. It struck me as sad that something so beautiful is also so unusual, and I wondered about ways to develop such happiness. I am not sure my idea would work, but just thinking about it makes me feel frisky.

If the parent who practices with the child would pick one day of each week in which to only have fun with the child, think of what could happen. It would be up to the imagination of the parent to find creative ways of having fun, but what really matters is that the parent and child actually **enjoy** this special day together. There should be no set pattern as to when this day occurred in the week, and the child should not know that such a thing was in the mind of the parent. But all of a sudden he would have a day in which laughter, fun and joy were spread around the whole lesson. How surprised he would be.

At first this day would have to be well planned, because having a thoroughly enjoyable practice might not be such a natural procedure. Gradually though, the parent would find such a time happening more easily and spontaneously.

The obvious result is that the child learns faster because of the air of fun and surprises involved. Gradually this pleasantness would help to form a very positive experience in the child's mind about practice.

The result that isn't so obvious however, is that the parent learns about how to have an enjoyable practice. It is much too easy to think that when we practice we must get down to business and really get serious, and then we spoil any joy that could have been in the practice. As the parent learns more and more how to practice with joy, the pleasant feeling would gradually sift into all practices.

The thought of seeing the mother and child laughing and hugging after the lesson will keep me thinking of ways to bring joy to learning and life.

Beauty

Today, when only the birds were awake, after a gentle spring rain, when the sun was just starting to peek over the mountains, I went to sit in the park in front of the school. The spring flowers were blooming, the shaped trees were green, the lilacs were full, and the smell in the early morning was gentle and beautiful. Here, in the park, I had a little party with the trees and birds and flowers. Dr. Suzuki often talks about studying nature, and says that when we begin to understand and appreciate nature it will show in everything that we do. I don't really understand that, but I can tell you that the birds and trees and flowers are wonderful company at an early morning party.

Thought At The End Of My Stay

It is quite a privilege to be here, able to see Suzuki often, and observe him. When I first came, I often read *Nurtured by Love* in the lobby of the school. I was often amazed by what this man said, and moved to tears by his love for people. Several times when I was feeling the depth of love expressed in his book, he would happen to walk through the lobby and say a few words to me.

At first I was a bit ashamed to say that this book, or the man had moved me to tears, but then I saw Suzuki at the annual grand concert. He watched the thousands of children playing beautifully, he heard the singing, and saw the joy on the faces of the children. When the children played the Bach Concerto, he started to cry. He said to the people sitting around him, "When they play from the heart so beautifully, I always cry." From the heart. That seems to be the key. It comes out in Suzuki's book, and it comes out in peoples' music.

In *Nurtured by Love*, Suzuki talks of places and things, I have had the good fortune to see and experience. Oddly enough, little is added by experiencing them because Suzuki's point is so clearly made in his book. There is so much about teaching and living in this book, and it is all expressed by the title.

I cannot say that living here has been particularly easy. On the contrary, the physical and mental adaptations that are required are severe. But I can say that "from the heart" has made it all worthwhile.

The Last Letter From Japan
(May 28, 1978, Matsumoto)

There has been much excitement in Matsumoto recently because of a new department store that has just opened. One of my American friends said to me, "Now we know what it must have been like when the first big stores hit the frontier towns in America."

For the grand opening of this store the management brought in help from Tokyo. Coming from an international city, they could speak English. I spent a large part of the day just walking around, having clerks come up to me and ask if they could help me in English. I would ask some inane question about the color or size of something, and they were happy to be so helpful. Many things were printed in two languages — they seemed to be imported — so I could actually tell what was inside the packages in this store. Eventually, I actually bought something, and was very pleased. It was exciting.

Even more exciting was a special section of the store which sold hamburgers and french fries! It seemed ironic. Several months ago, after being here for six months, I took a train to Nagoya, which is about four hours away, where I ate a McDonald's hamburger, a Pizza Hut pizza, and some Kentucky Fried Chicken. I slept in a real bed in a heated room and sat on a Western-style toilet. After six months without all those things, it was just what I needed to get charged up again. It was well worth the time and money to have some feeling of home come to me.

Now I can get hamburgers in Matsumoto! Granted, they aren't made from beef (the exact content is undetectable) and the French fries are made from powdered potatoes. But who cares?

As I was standing in line for my hamburger, a girl behind

the counter said to me in English, "Can I help you?" I was so astonished, I could not speak for several moments. I had spent several minutes constructing my order in Japanese with great difficulty. After all that struggle I became confused and couldn't think of how to say it in English. So, I gave her my order in Japanese.

As I walked out the door and down the street, eating my hamburger, another foreigner happened to be walking toward the store and came running up to me. He grabbed me, shook me by the shoulders, and said, "Where did you get that hamburger!?" He was trying to get mine away from me, I think, but I was very elusive. I took him and showed him where he too could get a hamburger and French fries.

Granted, I am in Japan, and should really be able to speak Japanese, so I certainly don't want to make it sound like the Japanese people should speak English. But I must say, that the day we can get a hamburger, French fries, and a milkshake in English, in Matsumoto, then I am ecstatic. It saves a whole day's travel and $50.00 besides.

Last week, some Japanese people took me to a restaurant with a beautiful Japanese garden. I noticed several kinds of fish in the pond, besides the customary goldfish. My friends told me that this restaurant was famous for its fresh fish. Can you imagine my surprise, however, when the *chef* left the kitchen and went into the garden with a big dipping net? He promptly netted a catch of fish and went back into the kitchen. Shortly thereafter, our waiter brought us a plate full of broiled, whole fish for snacks.

In just a few weeks I will be back in America again, after living in a country where I have seen so many different things, and have come to realize the huge, if not total effect that our environment has on us. My world will never be quite the same. For one year, I have lived in a place where much that I have learned to believe over the years is out of place. What I thought was the only right way of acting, speaking, and thinking, is indeed, only one of the ways. I have seen things previously unimaginable, which have made me know that, in fact, I know nothing.

Above all else, I have seen one thing that can cut through

cultural barriers, opposing views of politeness, age, language, boredom, fear, loneliness, and anything else. This one "miracle worker" is love.

The Real Constant

I once heard a saying that struck me as humorous. As often happens, once I had heard it, it seemed to appear often from that time on. When I got to Japan I was amused to find that this saying is a major premise there.

When I first heard this saying, I began to study it for its significance. Soon I was convinced of its accuracy, and also that the more significant part of the premise was only implied. This implication made me uncomfortable, and as my discomfort started to build, I had to face it directly. I finally realized that I could not fight the premise. Actually, that was part of the implication.

The premise to which I refer is: "The only constant is change." The implication is that we can fight change, but we cannot stop it. Over the years I have learned to let this concept help me to grow and to reduce emotional fatigue and worry. But even now I sometimes get angry with myself because I find that I am resisting it, or have forgotten its significance. However, when the fatigue and concern grow strong enough, the saying makes itself heard to me again. I often wish that I didn't have to keep learning the same lessons over and over.

This whole business weighed very heavily on me when I was in Japan; for what I once took to be facts, solid concepts, or institutions all began to have a different validity in that time and place. If I tried to keep my old concepts amid the pressures of new knowledge, I became unbearably burdened.

This is all an introduction to the fact that I have moved to a different place in America. The countryside is different, the customs are different, and so many things have changed in significance and importance, not only from Japan to America, but within America.

Often in my life I have had to explain the name of the city of Mankato, Minnesota. It is an Native American word that means "blue earth." This is because the soil there is so deep, rich, fertile and black that it is almost blue. When I lived there, of course, this carried no real significance for me. I assumed that all dirt looked like that. I do remember that visitors to Mankato would often giggle about "blue earth", but then I knew that people giggle about many things that are strange to them.

When I went to Japan, I discovered that there the earth isn't black at all. But so many things were different that I could accept, and even almost expect the earth to be of a different color. However, can you imagine my surprise on moving to Kentucky to find that the earth here is of a reddish color and the grass is blue!

As a matter of fact, there are so many things that are different here, just a small distance from Minnesota. I am happy and thankful for this. It is such a wonderful aid in looking at things with fresh interest. It helps keep me in awe and wonder, discovering new things every day. Looking at normal and mundane things with fresh eyes makes life itself inspiring.

Whether in the land of blue earth or blue grass, a tree never stops changing; it is always growing.

Can You Believe It?

Before I left America for Japan, a dear friend told me, "You will have some culture shock to go through." I didn't say anything, but just smiled. I thought to myself, "I have been studying about Japan quite a bit, and, more importantly, I have been learning not to be affected by changes." Those were my thoughts. Luckily I didn't speak them.

While in Japan, I had at least one major shock every day. There were aftershocks and minor shocks too, much like an earthquake. The shocks were only realizations that the concepts, objects, or beliefs of an entire people could be something completely different from what I once believed.

Often the shocks were small, like when I found that it is rude not to make huge swishing noises when eating soup, or that it would greatly embarrass a host if I were to clean my plate. These are small things taken separately; but experienced every day for months, they begin to make fundamental changes. I suspect that I am unaware of what the changes are, except for one: I have noticed that I really look at things around me now.

I can remember getting a letter from an American friend who had gone back to the States from Japan about a month before me. She wrote that she was experiencing severe culture shock and having a very difficult time speaking English, even though we both spoke only English in Japan. "Everyone talks so fast, and they take speaking so for granted," she wrote. "They don't even watch to see if the listener is listening or comprehending what they are saying." Again, I was greatly amused by her comments. After all the shocks I had gone through, certainly I wouldn't be shocked in my own country.

How vividly I remember the thrill of landing at O'Hare airport and hearing the announcements and pages being made in English. I was so thrilled that I called in and had myself paged just to hear my name spoken in American English. I hid behind a pillar to see if I would answer the page, but I never did see me go to the desk.

I am astonished that every day I am shocked now in America. How strongly I am in the habit of realizing that things might not be as they seem, and that what a person says or does might mean something very different to each of us. I have gotten into the habit of assuming that I may not completely understand what a person is saying or doing. Sometimes I get angry at myself because of my constant scrutiny, my feelings of watching so carefully, and of not understanding things. But then I remember what I've experienced and remind myself, "After what you have seen of other cultures, customs, morals and religions, how can you really take things for granted?" Maybe my feelings of confusion are good to keep, for they have greatly improved my power of observation, and also help me communicate with people. I can't take it for granted that someone understands what I am saying. I must use all of my senses, not just my voice, when I talk to find if I am really communicating. I realize how often I misinterpret an action or statement because the other person is coming from a base so different from mine. Dr. Suzuki speaks of the shock he had upon realizing that all Japanese children speak Japanese. Well, my shock came when I found out that the dogs in Japan don't know what "Sit!" means. Japanese dogs speak Japanese, too.

My days in America are filled with wonder and awe now.

The first time I rode in a car here, I had to close my eyes. I thought we were on the wrong side of the street and were going to be hit for certain. When I tried to walk across the street I was nearly run over. Of all things, the car had come from my left and not from my right!

The first time I went into a grocery store in Matsumoto, I looked for half an hour and came out of the store empty-handed. I had not been able to find one item that I could recognize. After being back in the States for several days, a friend took me to a grocery store. It seemed very strange to see both men and women shopping for groceries. I had forgotten that men do that in America. I did remember shopping carts, though I had not seen one for over a year. But I was quite taken aback when someone started packing my groceries for me and carried them out to the car. I had grown so used to the daily shopping concept and seeing people take their groceries home on bicycles, that I didn't remember at first that people here shop by the week.

I can remember the joy of reading the label on a can of soup. I think I looked around the store for almost and hour, at times close to tears, seeing all this food that I knew, and remembering how I had taken it all for granted before.

Every day I am astonished by what I see. I think, "Gosh, if only people could realize what is around them every day. If only people could see with fresh eyes. Just imagine how people would appreciate each other and the world."

I suppose my reaction will fade in time, along with my "fresh eyes." I guess, sadly, that my feelings are just a stage of culture shock after all.

I Am Eager To Learn

It is now over a year since I returned from Japan. It is hard to believe how greatly a few months there affected me. I am also astonished at how gradually I am learning the lessons from Japan. I don't understand how I can keep learning things about Japan and myself so long after the fact. I only know that I still find major lessons from there, as if they are slowly seeping into me.

Recently I realized that there is a huge difference in the philosophy of teaching between East and West. I realized it by teaching here and watching other teachers around America. I knew something was vastly different, but couldn't put my finger on what it was for many months. Somehow, I knew we were working too hard to teach the children. It wasn't nearly as easy for the teacher or student here. The lessons were much longer, yet the forward momentum was not as great. There just seemed to be so much teaching!

I got a hint of the difference when an advanced student came to me and asked for help in fingering a piece. "Ah ha," I thought. "What is this?" I couldn't get everything to click in my mind until later when I was reviewing a lesson I had had with Suzuki. I had memorized a piece, but had inverted several sections. Suzuki let me play the whole piece, and we worked on several musical points. After he was done teaching me he went and looked at his book and said, "Ah, yes; you have made a new arrangement of this piece." Then we bowed and the lesson was over.

Of course that was all that was needed. I went home, listened to the tape of my lesson, studied the music, found the mistake and corrected it. I felt gratified in doing so, as if I had made my own discovery, and had helped myself, not as though I had been forced to change something.

I was a teacher trainee, and knew there were certainly differences between me and younger students. So I researched how the other Japanese teachers taught children. I found then, and understand even more now, that their teachers really don't teach at all. They just prepare the students to learn!

A Japanese teacher never does for the student what the student could do for himself.

Of course, there were times when a teacher thought a student could do something, and it didn't get done properly. It happened between Suzuki and me several times too. But I didn't get scolded or reprimanded. Neither did Suzuki help me solve the problem. He just emphasized the same problem in a different way and let me find out how to solve it. The first problem I solved took two months. Suzuki just kept re-emphasizing the same thing many different ways until I finally solved it. Talk about a patient man!

Gradually, as I began to catch on to the problems and the

solutions faster, Suzuki made the problems harder to solve and hid them more expertly. I had not only to find more difficult solutions, but had to become a more astute observer even to locate the one point.

I wonder. He did all this so expertly that it has taken me a year to uncover his method. Perhaps I didn't become so astute after all!

Run That By Me Again, Please!

When I first heard a tape of one of my lessons with Suzuki, I was dismayed at how I sounded. I learned so much from the tape, however, that I listened anyway. Soon I began to realize that things were changing in my playing, unconsciously, from hearing the tapes.

The most valuable thing was that I was able to attend my lesson as a non-participant. When I was actually involved in the lesson, I did not hear much difference between what Suzuki did and what I did. But when I heard it on tape, I could tell a great deal of difference, and could work toward his example with better understanding.

The difference in tone was so dramatic that it was impossible to miss. For a long time I thought it was the difference in our violins. But during one lesson, acting on an impulse, I reached over and traded violins with Suzuki, giving him mine to demonstrate with. He laughed with delight, played my violin, and gave it back to me. I then tried to play with the same depth of sound, and assumed my tone was just like his. But everyone in the room started to giggle. Listening to the tape afterward, I too had to laugh. The tone that Suzuki made was so much deeper and richer that it was difficult to believe we had both played on the same instrument.

Recently, here at home, I had a high school student who taped her lesson every week. I could tell by her progress, however, that she wasn't listening to the tape. Each week I asked her to listen to it, but she never seemed to find the time.

Finally, at one lesson, unknown to her, I tried an experiment. She played a scale for me and I taped it. Without comment I rewound the tape, played it back to her, and asked her to play the same scale again. The second time she played much better than the first time. I played that back to her, still without comment. The third time she sounded like a different player altogether. When I questioned her, however, she was not aware of any change at all. So, I played back the entire series of three scales to her. She was astonished, and joined her mother and me in a good round of laughter.

The next week there was a huge leap in her development. When I asked if she had listened to the tape, she blushed and said, "Yes. And I even caught my mother red-handed listening to it just as I came home from school!"

A Point Of View

Some time ago I made a startling discovery while teaching my students in a group lesson. I was playing a solo and asked the students to find what I did wrong. They were very good at picking out the bad things. As a matter of fact, every one of the children found something wrong with my playing. Some even found things that I had not done wrong on purpose!

I suppose that I should have been delighted at their perception, but what I found instead was a strange feeling in me of "wrongness." I even had a feeling of dejection, even though this was only a game. It made me wonder how children must feel when a teacher or parent finds wrong points when it is not a game.

I decided to conduct an experiment; I thought of a new game. Instead of having the children pick out my bad points, I asked them to find the good points. At first they couldn't do it. They had been thinking about looking for what was wrong for so long, that they couldn't switch their point of view. Finally, after a few tries, they were able to find something good, even though I often played in a grotesque way.

Some amazing things started to happen then. The whole atmosphere of the room changed. It seemed to have a light and happy feeling in it — even though this was all only a game! I must admit that even I felt better not having the students tell me what I had done wrong. But the biggest surprise came when I noticed the change in the students when they played their solos. They seemed to be able to play with new freedom. With the knowledge that their peers were not looking for bad points, but good points, they felt a new surge of confidence and joy in their playing.

It seemed like such a good idea, that I played the game with the parents too. Gosh, did they have a hard time switching from bad point thinking to good point thinking. But eventually they too were able to make the switch. After several weeks of playing this new game, I had a delightful reward. I noticed that parents had started telling their children the good points about their solos automatically after the group lesson was over.

Over a period of months, this trend took hold more and more within the families. At one recital, I looked out over the audience with indescribable joy. I realized that we didn't have an audience full of music critics, but an audience of people unconsciously supporting the performers.

Several times this past summer, while teaching at workshops, I have asked students to play solos for each other. Often I was surprised to find a general reluctance to play for their peers. So I tried the "good point" game. Then I asked for volunteers to play solos again. In every case someone was willing to play. After the first student played, I asked each student to find some good point. This led to some new interest in playing for each other, and invariably, by the end of the week, every student requested to play a solo. Nothing really changed except the point of thinking.

Reunion In America

Recently I experienced a heartwarming reunion. It was not exactly what I had expected it to be; in fact, it was much deeper and better than I had anticipated.

You can well imagine that, after living for a year in a foreign city where there were only ten other foreigners, and where we represented Western culture, that friendships would develop between us. While going through difficult and wonderful times together, supporting and sharing with each other, all studying under a man like Suzuki, our bonds of friendship became quite deep. Knowing all of these things I still was not prepared for what we found together in America.

Not all of the foreigners present were Americans, and not all of our group were here. As close as we became in Japan, we knew that when we left Suzuki we might never see each other again, and the chances of all of us again being together in the same place at the same time were almost nil. It was a sad, but beautiful thing to feel at the time. Even now, when someone mentions the name of a country where I have a friend, I feel somehow closer to that country. It seems like this must be the "small earth" that Suzuki often talked of.

Anyway, this summer several of us met here in America. We felt unified immediately. We didn't need to talk and get caught up on events to feel close again. We just "knew" each other. This much I expected, really, although it seemed deeper than I had known before. It was almost a relief to be with these friends, for we knew intimately of one of the major events in each other's lives. We understood much about each other and the kinds of feelings we were going through after returning to our home countries. We laughingly agreed that what we thought at the time were some incredible hardships, had in fact deepened our lives greatly. The hardships were almost humorous in retrospect.

I got my biggest surprise when I went to a lecture given by several of these friends about their "Japanese experience." I was astonished! They talked of the same kinds of things and feelings that I felt so deeply too. They spoke with a certain reverence that I felt so much a part of. They spoke of Japanese things with the curious English that one acquires by being around Suzuki and living in Japan. We had never discussed these things; we just mutually shared them.

Of course, we all realized how much Japan had affected us only after we returned to our home countries, so we didn't talk of

these things as they were happening — we were too involved in
the situation. But to find that we shared so many common
insights that we each had felt to be unique was deeply revealing.

Most surprising of all, however, was hearing these people
talk about Suzuki. It was only at this time that I realized that even
in Japan we rarely, if ever, spoke about Suzuki to one another.
Back in America we all seemed to have plenty of stories to tell to
other people, to let them know about Suzuki. But it seemed that
we people who had been with Suzuki never spoke about him. I
could not understand this, and finally talked with some of these
friends about it. We all agreed that we held Suzuki in such a
special place in our hearts, had such a reverence for his spirit and
love that it was not conceivable to talk about him to each other.
We were secure in the knowledge that we all had Suzuki's love so
strongly that there was no need to discuss it. He had made us all
so eager to learn and teach that it was pointless to discuss his
method. And then, Suzuki is Suzuki — there just doesn't seem to
be anything to say about him to people who know him.

Our lives were all immeasurably enriched by this man —
indeed the whole world is. I wonder what it will be like to be
with Suzuki in Japan next time?

I Know A Person

Many things, places and people influenced me greatly during my stay in Japan just by their presence. Often now, back in America, I receive little flashes of insight that tell me even more about events that happened in Japan. A few days ago, looking through my pictures, I found one of a person that made me think about dedication. It made me think about a person who has helped so many scores of people, and they don't even know it.

This person lives in a foreign country, and gets to speak her native tongue only a few times each year, if that. She has done this for over 40 years. She lives in a small mountain town where foreigners are a great oddity. Every day she is looked upon as someone strange, and yet every day she continues to help people in her way, and to give support to her husband.

She once told me about an event that happened about a decade ago. Her husband had written a book, and many of his ideas were beginning to reach foreign countries. This book could help many people understand his ideas. So a professional translator was asked to translate the book. He studied the book for weeks and finally said, "I am sorry. This book is too difficult for me to translate into English." Another translator was contacted. He finally said, "These ideas cannot really be said in English." It looked as though there was no hope of getting the book translated for her husband.

This woman was of a different opinion, though. She could speak Japanese and even recognize some of the Japanese characters, so she set out on her project. To read the thousands of characters, each meaning a thought, not a word, and each thought varying according to context, meant that she had to look up each character in a dictionary and then, finally, compose it all into the more concrete English. Her native tongue being German, this task is beyond my imagination, but she was determined to do it. When this woman determines to do something, she does it!

She kept this all a secret from her husband, often working until very late into the night. Sometimes her husband would ask, "What are you doing so late at night?" She avoided answering the question.

Finally, after many months of this struggle, the book was finished. She gave it to her husband, and it was published in English under the title *Nurtured By Love*.

Of course, the woman is Mrs. Suzuki. Her struggle to help Suzuki — the hardships, the work and the trauma — reaches epic proportions.

I was fortunate enough to be in Japan on their 50th wedding anniversary. Suzuki said to her, "The second 50 years will be better than the first 50."

The Sparkle Of Interest

During my stay in Japan, Suzuki asked me to work on a difficult project. It took most of my time and energies for weeks. I skipped meals, classes, and lost considerable amounts of sleep. It was one of the most difficult and demanding projects I had ever attempted. The day I finally completed the project and gave it to him, he said something I can never forget. He said, "Yes, thank you. We must change the world."

What a very strange thing to say, especially for a music teacher! How could the world possibly be changed by what we are doing?

I am thinking back a number of years to when I taught in the public schools, and recall the discussions that I had with a variety of teachers then. It was lucky, I thought, that teachers who taught kindergarten through third grade really preferred to do just that. They said that at those ages the children are so vitally interested in everything. It is so easy to teach them, all you have to do is put the right things around them in the right way, and they learn.

The teachers who taught older children said that they couldn't possibly teach young children. Their minds go so easily from one thing to another that you have to watch them too closely. Older children can work on their own and respond better in groups. It is true that they don't, as a rule, have the keen interest in every thing, but the trade off is worth it.

The more I looked, the more I saw the keen interest and bright eyes of the children dull as they became "more stable or older." It was a sad thing to see that fire grow smaller, and I wondered why it happened. Could it be that the way we teach contributes to a reduction in their desire to learn, or is it just a sign of growing up?

Teaching General Music in a junior high school is an ideal way to observe children in a place that can dull the eyes' sparkle. Here is a job that strikes fear into teachers with even the stoutest hearts. Perhaps, as a lesson in human growth and development, all adults should be required to spend a day in a junior high or high school. I think that many people would be astonished, some would be frightened, and some would be furious. I guess that everyone would be greatly affected.

I have had the great fortune of meeting and working with people in many countries who are drawn together by the fundamental philosophy of the Suzuki method: *"For the happiness of all children."* I have worked with people from the ages of three to sixty. I have watched, listened, and been repeatedly astonished. These people have some qualities that make them unlike other people in some ways. They all have an interest that seems to grow keener with time, not duller. There is respect for human beings and things. There seems to be a quality about these people that bespeaks personal growth.

Lately I have been watching teenagers intently. I have been amazed to see that teenage Suzuki students are unusual. They are confident. They still have a desire to learn. They are kind and respectful. It is a treat to be around such people. They help us understand what Suzuki means when he says the world can be changed by helping each person develop a noble being and a higher spirit. Person by person the world will change.

"Yikes It's Cold . . ."

I have recently been involved in some discussions about the question of child behavior, and what to do with little rascals who create havoc in class. For years I have seen instances of young children controlling their parents completely. I have been in situations where children have controlled me for a while. I have attended many lectures and read many books on discipline, and yet somehow they did not provide me with the answer I was looking for. After many years, I think I am getting close to an answer, but I am still searching for ways in which to apply what I have found. I expect that to be true for many more years.

I grew up on a lake. Almost every day I could be found in some form or another floating in the lake. My favorite way of floating was in a canoe. It was so silent and light and responsive. It was so easy to observe deer, fox, ducks and other wildlife while in the canoe. Somehow it made me feel closer to nature, a part of nature.

In our lake there were sandbars, large rocks, logs, and islands. I found it best to avoid running into these things with the canoe. I also noticed that if I was observant and caught the problem early enough, I could avoid any hazard without changing the rhythm of my stroke. I merely needed a small deflective push in my stroke and the problem was avoided. If I was not watching, I might find myself almost upon an obstacle. In this case I would desperately try to turn at short range, perhaps even needing to back paddle. The energy required to avoid the collision was very great and often not effective. There were several holes in my canoe that needed to be repaired.

If the lake was calm, the trick to good travel was a smooth, even rhythm and a watchful eye that could detect trouble early enough that a mere flick of the wrist could avoid the problem. All of this could then be balanced with a rich enjoyment of the lake, the motion, and the rhythm of the paddle in the water.

If there was a strong wind I had to be much more careful to observe natural laws. Travel could still be enjoyable, but only if I observed and went in the correct manner. It was impossible to take a direct course into the wind and waves; an angular course was the only way to go. A few tries proved that my only choice was to tack or to expend all my energy and still not be where I wanted to be. When going at an angle to the wind it was necessary to change my position in the canoe. Otherwise the wind would catch the tip and overturn everything. Once I refused to do this and ended up swimming home. These tactics were not only the easiest in the long run, but indeed the only effective means to move.

When I learned to let the canoe work with me, when I saw how to go with the natural processes, then I began to let the rhythm carry us both. This was when I began to really enjoy the lake, the canoe, the rocks, the islands, and the logs. All the books and teaching couldn't help me get to this point. It took years of study and work on my part. It also took being dumped out of the canoe into the cold water a number of times.

I find that it is important for someone to have a grip on the steering paddle. Usually only the smallest of efforts is needed to keep moving on a proper course. Splashing about wildly only gets us wet.

I guess the teacher of the moment must control the canoe — no matter how subtly. A canoe with no rudder runs aground.

Was Something Squeezed In Or Out?

I was startled during a lesson not long ago, and then rewarded with results that helped me greatly. I was teaching a young child and said something that caused him frustration, which came out as anger at me. I was very startled and tried to keep my composure, but was having difficulty. I was unable to reach the child through our mutual frustrations, and the situation was rapidly deteriorating. I was quite at a loss as to what to do, when the parent came to the child and whispered something in his ear. Suddenly, the child put down the violin and gave me a hug.

You cannot imagine how taken aback I was by this gesture. I was as amazed as when he suddenly flared up. The relief I felt could have been measured with a barometer. I knew that there was no way words could have gotten us out of the dreadful situation, indeed, they only seemed to make it worse. But that hug cut through the impossibleness of the situation for both of us. Thank heaven for the parent's inspiration.

I perceived long ago that I could give hugs to people when words couldn't help, but I never thought the remedy would work on me. That hug cut through all the barriers and hurts and seemed to say "through everything and anything our relation-ship is what is important." Of course that is a very bad translation, because what the hug said cannot be said in words. I am beginning to think, though, that those kinds of hugs are really medicine!

What They See Is What They Get

Children are very demanding. I feel that the biggest demand they make on us is honesty. If honesty isn't coming out, they go in after it.

The first clue I had to this came when I discovered that the Japanese have a curious way of asking important questions. When a Japanese person wants to find out the answer to a question, he does not actually ask, as Westerners do. Instead, he creates a circumstance to which a person can respond with the fullness of his beliefs. Because people can say anything, whether they believe it or not, such non-verbal answers are much more accurate, it seems. Maybe this approximates our Western saying: "Actions speak louder than words."

The insight I gained from this knowledge led me to watch situations speak. I was fascinated to find that children live their whole lives this way. They seem to sense when our words do not fit our actions or feelings. When they see this happen, they act in ways which make us act out our true feelings.

For instance, I have been in situations where we adults act calm but, in fact, are far from calm inside. Children sense this somehow, and create situations in which we adults can no longer act calm but must act in the way that we really feel.

The odd thing is that the children don't seem to mind that I am agitated if my actions match my feelings. They do mind, however, if I lie with my actions. I dread teaching if I am not calm and centered, for the children fidget and do everything they can to make me admit that I am actually churning inside. They can spot me a mile away. If I am about to praise them, it had better be what I really feel inside, because if I am insincere they will somehow sense it.

Kids are personality experts. They can peer into a person and respond fully to what is really there.

"Look Out, Here Comes Timmerman!!!"

For a time in my life I was a forklift driver in a large factory. It was wonderful preparation for becoming a violin teacher. Nowadays my job is just about the same as driving the forklift — just as exciting, and just as dangerous.

You may not know that the most practical way to drive a "jeep", as they are called affectionately, is to go backwards. Most times, loads are too large to see over or around. So to proceed in a factory full of moving people and objects, it was necessary to back up. First I had to go forward and pick up the load, which often required a great deal of dexterity with the forks. Then I would back up several blocks to the assembly lines and set it down on exactly the right spot.

It was my job to keep three assembly lines supplied with parts. If I made a mistake, or was too slow in bringing parts, the line would have to shut down. The reasons for my not bringing the parts were never asked; either the line was running or it was down. When it got shut down, the anger that was expressed towards me was not of the most subtle nature. I never enjoyed hearing the people express their anger, so I usually raced the engine of my jeep. Not only did that cover the voices, but soon the people were so concerned with all the noise they forgot to shout at me any more.

In the beginning, I thought the only way to keep the line up was to keep my jeep running full speed. I even worked during the break periods because I couldn't keep up. This meant going quite fast with some dangerous loads. One time I was carrying a heavy load of sheet metal and had to stop suddenly for a pedestrian, who happened to be the factory superintendent. It is a good thing he was watching, because the metal slid off, sheet over sheet, and flew quite a distance. Had he not jumped clear, it would have cut the man off at his knees. Another time I was carrying a tall load of heavy wooden crates, going backwards at full speed. As I rounded a curve, I heard a scream. My load had flown off the jeep. Several people had to dive out of the way to avoid being crushed.

I began to think that there must be a more effective and safer way to do this. Then I learned the trick to driving a jeep. It is, "Never run empty." Always carry something, even if you have to make a small detour. In the long run it is the fastest and only way. In other words, make every move count. Then, slow down, don't hurry, and it works.

Almost everything transferred to teaching children. I still spend most of my day backing up. First I must catch the interest of a student. Then I must back up just a little ahead of the student. To keep interest and develop momentum in the child, I don't push forward.

Children have a way of racing their engines to prevent us from coming to the center of a tough situation. It works for them too.

Children can be crushed as easily as it is to turn a corner too fast. They don't know how to jump out of the way.

I guess I could say, "Don't hurry; never run empty; make every move count; keep your tanks full." Then we keep our production lines up and running.

Artificial Living

I can remember the days, not long ago, when I spent so much time watching television that I felt like part of the family on the screen. After work, I sat in front of the screen and even ate meals there. Sometimes I would arrange my schedule around the time of a certain show. When someone made an allusion to an advertisement or show, I was right up with them. I could sing the jingles for just about any product.

Then I left for Japan. Of course, for me to own a set there, or even to watch TV, would have been out of the question, not only for financial reasons, but because I could not understand Japanese. Without my being conscious of it at all, TV was deleted from my life. Oddly enough, I didn't miss it. There were too many things to see, too many things to do, and so many adjustments to make! I was completely occupied just by living.

Since I had to walk wherever I went, I began to notice flowers and plants and trees. They became more interesting to me, and I noticed minute changes in them from day to day as I walked the same route several miles to school. I started to notice animals and birds in the city. I travelled slowly enough to appreciate buildings and structures. I could hear the water running beside the road and smell the plants as I walked by. I sometimes heard someone practicing *koto* in one house, flute in another, piano in another, violin down the road.

Of course, things got carried to extremes for me there. I didn't have a radio or newspaper, so I became isolated from outside events. But the major change was that I was unreached by advertising for a year! I hadn't noticed, until it was gone, how much we are constantly bombarded with advertising and other things clamoring for our attention. I was pleased at how much clearer I felt without all that nonsense.

I must admit that there were times when I was distressed over the change. Boredom, fatigue and loneliness were my companions many times as I lived that new lifestyle. But gradually I noticed that my life seemed fuller and richer. Instead of watching other people live their lives, I was having to live mine myself. I had the time to do things that I needed and wanted to do. My ability to live more fully was developing out of necessity.

Once or twice I did watch a little TV. I understood only a fraction of the Japanese, but found the advertisements very catchy, even though I couldn't understand them. The clincher for me, though, was watching a John Wayne Western dubbed into Japanese. When he sauntered up to the bar and said in a Japanese voice I couldn't recognize as his, "Excuse me, could I please have a whiskey?" I burst out laughing and had to leave the room. It was just too much.

Nowadays, here in America, I hear children say, "I don't want my lesson on Saturday — that is when cartoons are on." Then I am reminded of how it felt to be affected like that and living my own life that way. I am saddened to hear children talk like that, or to see anyone live around the screen.

I have come to believe that television stunts growth even more than coffee. Of course, I am working hard to get this article done now so I can go shopping for a TV . . .

The Silent Wisdom Of Children

There have been times when people ask me what I do for a living that I think I should answer, "I take lessons from children." It seems to me that children contain the wisdom of the universe in their eyes and heart.

It has happened to me several times that, when I look at a baby, I have become lost somewhere. After a timeless time, when I find where I am, I feel like I have looked into the very face of infinity, and am changed deeply. How is it possible that these tiny babies contain eternity?

Several days ago I was grocery shopping. Seated in a cart was a charming little girl. As I walked by she turned and looked at me and said, "You're nice." Good heavens! I was so startled, and so happy. We started to have a delightful conversation. This child had such sparkling eyes, and was radiating joy and happiness. Soon, her mother came back, and of course we, being adults and strangers, didn't speak to each other. Just as I was leaving, the little girl turned to her mother and said, "Say 'hello' to the man."

Well, we adults both laughed and talked inanely as strangers do, but somehow without the freedom of the child. This little girl spread such joy in her wake that I found myself whistling to the "Muzak" as I walked out.

Of course, this little girl will have to learn that we don't talk to strangers. And she will have to learn what things are proper to say, and what things can't be said. And she will find out that you cannot say, "You're nice," to people you don't know. I just hope that I meet her several more times before she learns all of these adult things.

In Japan there were some children who lived near my house, which was close to the Suzuki school and to their elementary school. These children were my best teachers for many things. They would repeat words time after time, until I could finally say them, and then they would say them more times so that I could remember the words in Japanese. Then I would say the words in English, and they remembered them after only a few repetitions. They taught me many other things too, things crucial to living. Somehow they rearranged my concept of what is important in life.

Often I would be on my way somewhere and they would see me. They would swarm around me and ask where I was going, which was one thing I could understand in Japanese. Of course, I could never tell them in Japanese, so they would get hold of my hands and coat and drag me to a park where we would play and play until I was completely worn out. Their laughter and joy was worth any delay. And since in Japan a person can never really be late for anything, I always got to my appointments "on time" but with my tummy full of warmth and laughter.

The children taught me how to skip rope to a Japanese rhyme. Then I held onto their hands and swung them around until I was too dizzy to stand. We had to play in the streets, of course, since there were no yards, and often adults would stand at a distance and watch us playing, but there was no way we could communicate with each other.

Most houses in Matsumoto are not locked, and there are specific customs to learn for entering someone's home. Usually a person enters the front hall area and shouts, "Excuse me!" until there is some response. It was very difficult for me to get used to not knocking, but actually entering the house first. One day my little friends saw me walking to my house, and they followed me to see where I lived. From that day on, at least once a day, a bunch would come into the house and shout, *"Kragu-San"*, my name in Japanese. I always tried to spend a few minutes with them whenever they came. One little three-year-old in particular would crawl on my lap, quite easily since I was sitting on the floor, and would begin to talk. I presume he was telling me a story, or about his day at nursery school, or something of the sort. Then he would ask me in Japanese, "Did you understand?"

"No", I answered honestly. So he would start all over and tell me the whole story again. He did this for several months, and as far as I could tell, never asked me why I couldn't understand him when he talked to me.

Sometimes I just couldn't take time for the youngsters that day, and I would pretend to be asleep under the *kotatsu* table. Since they could see me from the front hallway, they would then sneak away, sliding the door shut as quietly as thunder.

These children taught me about joy and playing and repetitions and a huge desire to learn that they have built in. They taught me how children and wise men tell time, with the hands always on "now." They taught me about acceptance without cultural barriers. They taught me about inhibitions, because they had none. Even as I write this I can see their eyes shining like bright stars. I can hear their laughter and giggles. I can almost hear their smiles. I can remember how it felt when they took me by the hand to lead me to something very important like a mud puddle, or a ball stuck on a roof.

I remember how I laughed at myself the first time I played with a three-year-old American girl who had just come to Japan. I played with this child for almost an hour before realizing that I could actually speak with her. What a colossal surprise, after eight months, to hear a child speak English, and with a Southern accent!

I'm Only Five You Know

Yesterday one of my most affectionate students came to her

lesson in a very stubborn mood. I'd never seen a youngster so determined as she stomped into my kitchen. Her mother told me, "She is having a stubborn mood today." I told her, "Don't worry; I know how to fix that."

I swooshed down and picked her up, expecting that she'd give me her usual warm response. Instead I felt that I was holding a board.

I told her I wouldn't put her down until I got a hug. She just stuck her lip out stubbornly, and I thought we were going to have a contest of wills. After five minutes she got so heavy that I had to sit down. So I sat on a stool and rocked her gently. After five minutes of that she started to warm up a bit. I told her mom to close her eyes, then I sneaked a hug from Julianne, which she returned.

I knew it was still pointless to try to have a lesson, so I asked her if I could play her violin. She brought it to me, and I played with the accompaniment tape for several minutes. At first it was hard to play on such a small violin, but I finally got the hang of it. Soon, she sat down on my couch.

I really began to play for her then, thinking she would soon want to play too. But I had closed my eyes, and before I knew it had played all of Volume One on her 1/10th size violin. When I opened my eyes, there was Julianne . . . asleep on her mother's lap.

Oh, how wonderful to see that. But I really didn't know what to do about the lesson. I told her mom to call me and schedule a "real lesson" later in the week.

That night the strangest thing happened. Julianne told her father, "Daddy, I had my very best violin lesson today!" Julianne, I think it was my very best lesson too.

Don't Stare, It's Not Polite

I suppose it really is true: staring can be offensive to some people. However, children tend to stare at certain kinds of things in different kinds of ways. I enjoy finding children who are staring at something; then I look too.

When children look at oddities I watch their faces. When a child looks at something that makes him feel good, his face shows it, and I want to try and catch that feeling too. I really think that children are better at picking up feelings than I am. It has always turned out that, when they get that certain look on their faces, whatever or whoever caused it makes me feel good too. In every case, so far, when kids and I are staring, whomever we are looking at hasn't felt offended, and I always feel good vibrations coming from that source. Perhaps I use the children as detectives to help me find people or things that give off pleasant vibrations.

The eyes of children have taught me a whole lot about trusting, and a whole lot of other things as well.

Anyway, if you ever hear someone say to a child, "Don't stare!" please don't watch me, because I'll be finding out what the child was looking at for myself.

A Reason To Teach

Last night I could not sleep well. Luckily for me, the moon was shining. So, in the middle of the night I sat under a tree, watching the moon and the fireflies celebrating life all around me. I thanked God that my life is spent working with children and families.

Earlier in the evening I passed by a room where children were sleeping. I went in and sat down on the bed of a five year old child. Without waking, he moved over and snuggled up to me. I rubbed his back and he curled around me even more. Accidentally my tears fell on his pillow. I realized that this child had not yet learned how to hate. He had not yet learned mistrust and disgust. His whole body flowed with love and trust, and he was as vulnerable as a new sprout just emerging from the earth.

I thought I knew what love was, but this child taught me in his sleep that I have just begun to learn about love. I still must unlearn how to judge and criticize things and people. I still must unlearn how to hate. I still must unlearn how to be closed to learning by thinking that I already know.

This child, however, doesn't need to unlearn these things. He already knows.

As I was going down the stairs from this youngster's bedroom, I met a ten year old girl. She had glorious long red hair. I began to say, "You have beautiful hair," and without thinking, I reached out to touch it. She slapped my hand and snapped, "Don't touch me! If you come near me I'll break your finger off!"

I was stung as if by a jellyfish. All I could say was, "My gosh, you have really hurt my feelings."

She looked at me strangely and said, "People hurt me every day, so why should I care about you?" Then she began to cry and ran up the steps.

These two events happened within minutes of each other. The combination sapped my strength.

I asked myself, "How is it possible to start out in life so loving and open and trusting as the first child, and then, in a short while, develop into another kind of being entirely?"

Then I realized that the environment creates the kind of human being that develops. Some parents love life and live life. Some parents teach how to judge and criticize life by doing the same to their children. I saw that it is how we live that teaches, not what we say.

The moon was shining. Luckily I could feel a circle of love. Still, for hours I pondered these things.

The fireflies all around me made me feel like I was in an ocean of something.

I went into the house and played the violin in the dark. Some tears fell on my violin.

Announcing A Contest . . .

I am looking fore a place in wich to hold a speling be!!! I wil anounce soon where it wil be held and what the prizez wil bee, as well as the moad of speling to be used. It may be a "Webster" or "Oxford" or sum other excepted but differnt norm. I wil bee the soul judge of the contest.

Not long ago I wrote an article about my spelling. I received many reactions from that article. Only in a few cases did I find that my self-revelation helped anyone catch the point I tried to make.

Responses ranged from saying that my spelling gave the impression of illiteracy, to nullifying the value of my articles, to the question, "Is it possible that your misspelling is a teaching device?"

In several cases someone did say, "I can see that I judge people by the cover and fail to see what is inside. I let myself get sidetracked by completely unimportant details. It has prevented me from fully appreciating some person or the work of some person. The scolding that I have done about the problem has indeed shut off the person from me."

The most valuable concept in my education has been: "If you find yourself in disagreement with another person, you must know that the person either knows more than you do or less — but you never know which." This concept has helped me to stay open and ready to learn from all around me and from people I thought at first had nothing to teach me.

I have come to believe that in Japan wise people make their wisdom less than obvious. This makes people more observant, for the other person must be studied very carefully in order to catch the significance. Open flaunting of wisdom or knowledge is not only offensive in Japan, but also wisdom or knowledge gained in this easy way does not stick as well as that which a person has to search for. Perhaps the concept that struck me years ago was developed in Japan.

Of course, it would be ludicrous for me to say there is any wisdom in my spelling. But, it makes a good story.

Beethoven, Mozart, Casals, Or God?

When I lived in Matsumoto a dear friend sent me a quotation from *Nurtured By Love*. At first the quote was something that only sounded nice. But as I observed Suzuki in his teaching, working and living, I began to sense that perhaps there was a great deal more importance in this quotation after all. The quotation is this:

> *The real essence of art turned out to be not something high up and far off. It was right inside my ordinary daily self. The very way one greets people and expresses oneself is art. If a musician wants to become a fine artist, he must first become a finer person. If he does this, his worth will appear. It will appear in everything he does, even in what he writes. Art is not in some far-off place. A work of art is the expression of a man's whole personality, sensibility, and ability.*[1]

I put a copy of that quotation on my wall. Every day for months, before I went outside, I read and thought about it.

One day, after I had been doing this for some time, Suzuki came up to me and said out of the blue, "Before we can express art and beauty, we must learn to see it in all of the things around us." He would often say to us, "Study nature. Go into the grape fields and see how the grapes express art and beauty." One of the students took him quite literally and had a house smack in the middle of a vineyard. To get to his house we had to crouch down and walk half a block with vines forming a roof over our heads!

Presently I spend much of each day trying to catch the beauty that is around me — the web of a spider, the feel of cloth, or the smell of the air. I think it is possible that all things contain beauty if we only seek it.

Last fall, after a long day of teaching, I and several others drove out into the countryside. We were quite exhausted. But suddenly we had an idea. We stopped the car and started tramping through an old, dried-up slough, still wearing our good teaching clothes. The cockleburs, stickers and weeds were up to our necks. The smell of the dry, dusty weeds was overpowering. There was nothing green and living in sight. The leaves were in various bright colors of dying and falling to the ground. In front of us was an ugly field of corn stubble. Behind us we could hear hunters shooting at pheasants. In front of us the sun began to set and color the sky.

As we spoke casually of the past day, the sunset suddenly caught us. Soon, the smell I had detested before held a certain majesty. The weeds almost touching my nose were studies in symmetry and beauty. The sunset turned into a symphony. The things around us became an ocean of sound. Instead of seeing colors changing in cloud patterns and birds gliding through the sky, we were suddenly engulfed in a symphony of colors, smells, and sound. For more than half an hour we stood without making the slightest sound or movement, transfixed.

As we walked back to the car, we still could not talk. I couldn't see if I was the only one with tears in my eyes, but when we were able to talk, we could only agree that we had shared a most magnificent performance, some kind of great and grand symphony.

Who had written the score to this beauty-filled work? Who had been the performer?

———

1. *Nurtured by Love* by Shinichi Suzuki, Exposition Press, Smithtown, NY, 1969.

The Eye Of The Beholder

One day in 1976, when I lived in Minnesota, I went to an art exhibit. Since it was autumn, most of the paintings and photographs were of fall scenes: colorful leaves on trees, great piles of leaves, children having leaf fights, children leaping into piles of raked leaves. There were photographs of old deserted barns and lonely trees. Somehow these things produced feelings of deep emotions and melancholy.

Some time later I was driving on a trip through several small towns and miles of farm country with field after field of corn stalks. As I entered a small town I thought to myself, "For gosh sakes, why don't the people clean up around here?" There were leaves blowing around everywhere, and the air was heavy with the inescapable smell of drying leaves and autumn dust. On the edge of town were some old buildings, unpainted and falling apart. I became quite disgusted with it all, even though it was a warm, beautiful Indian Summer day. I rolled up the windows, turned on the air conditioner, and drove on, thinking of what I would do to clean up such messes if I could.

Suddenly, an old barn, partially burned down, on a hill with a cornfield all around it, came into view. It was such an interesting sight that I stopped the car. One of the photographs in the art show I had seen was of this very barn. When I got out of the car I could immediately smell the dusty cornhusks blowing around in the field, and could hear the rustle of all this activity. I saw some wild pheasants eating spilled corn. It was an enthralling view and evocative of many deep thoughts on the beauty of nature and the cycles of life.

Then I was struck by the thought that this view that I fancied as being very picturesque was really little different from the scene in the small town that disgusted me. Both depicted and implied the same kinds of things to me. Why was I suddenly not disgusted but enchanted instead?

I sat down at the edge of the cornfield to think about this troubling matter. How could the same scene be both beautiful and disgusting? What did the artist possess that let him appreciate a scene that in real life I found offensive?

I sat in the stubble of corn for some time, but never did find the answer to that question. After all this time I still haven't reached any answers, but whenever I look at any setting, I am more and more able to see the beauty that is within the scene. I cannot explain what has changed within me, but I can say that I have found joy in looking at many strange things. Even within a single blade of grass there is so much beauty.

Whatever changed within me kept changing until it became so strong that I had to start photographing. I especially began to enjoy photographing things that I formerly would have thought disgusting, or at least uninteresting. This activity has helped me to simply appreciate.

Sometimes I chuckle when someone says to me, "Look at that awful mess over there." I remember I used to think the same thing.

Heart Tone

On one wall of Suzuki's studio is a single picture. This is a Japanese way of placing special emphasis on something. The photo is of Fritz Kreisler. A big share of the Suzuki Method of violin playing comes from the study that Suzuki did of Kreisler.

Almost all of the advanced literature that Suzuki teaches has been recorded by Kreisler, and he asks all of the students to listen to these recordings, just as he often asked me to listen to Kreisler.

For a long while I didn't make the effort to find these recordings, which are available in Japan, though almost impossible to find in the U.S. I knew that Kreisler's playing was considered old fashioned, and very much out of style, so I went on without hearing those recordings.

After some months of working on tonalization exercises with Suzuki, I got some extra incentive to listen to Kreisler. I was playing an exercise, and suddenly Suzuki jumped out of his chair and said, "Ah, so. Now you have one note like Kreisler!"

Ah, so indeed! I began to listen to Kreisler very diligently then, and after some time began to perceive something very special in his tone. In the beginning I was rather amused by the style, and my face was often wreathed in smiles. Because of the unusual playing, I wasn't really listening and missed the point. But when I began to understand the things in his tone that Suzuki was hinting at, I began to get very excited. There is a special inner beauty, a special gentleness, and a special wisdom in Kreisler's tone. All of these things together, perhaps, make up what Suzuki calls "heart tone."

I took a photograph of that picture, and then blended in one of Suzuki. Perhaps this picture seems strange to you. Or perhaps it suggests that Suzuki plays with the singing, sweet, powerful tone of Kreisler. On the other hand, perhaps the picture suggests nothing to you at all, and seems like only a wasted double exposure. But to me it suggests and reminds me of all that Suzuki talked about.

Perhaps the "Kreisler Highway" is more than a place on the violin.

What Kind Of Language Is This?

In a country where I couldn't understand words, I noticed that I could understand music. Music, it seems, cuts across barriers in our rational minds. It is a language that speaks to some other part of us. Still, it is a language. It needs practice and growth to be an effective language for us to use and understand.

If I think about music as a language to be learned, it becomes easier to see what kinds of things to put in the environment of children learning technical skills on an instrument. If you were being taught a new language, and the only exposure to it was the learning of pronunciation and vocabulary for 30 minutes each day, what kind of language would you develop? It would be difficult to be motivated if that new language was excluded from the other parts of your life, if it wasn't a natural part of life.

Have you ever heard anyone speak English that was learned from a book? It is the most stilted, lifeless, uninteresting communication you can imagine. We can understand it and use it for communication, but it is not a living language at all. If we do the same thing with music, it is not a living language either.

In speaking a language, we learn the living parts unconsciously: things like the rate or tempo, the inflections, the pauses, and many other nuances. That we do learn these things becomes apparent when we travel, for in different areas those nuances are different and indigenous. It may be possible to teach those things to children, but I think it is probably something that must grow within, naturally, from the environment.

This makes me realize how important it is for children to hear good music being played and enjoyed at home naturally, and how important it is to attend concerts and places where music is being enjoyed and expressed. Making music a part of the environment must be the most important factor in practicing. Then music is a language, alive and communicating to something within us.

Music Is Music

"As music teachers we have one of the greatest privileges there could be, for into the lives of our students we can bring the capacity to express and feel things which cannot be communicated in any other way. If we can truly give this to our students, we have given them one of the most wonderful gifts they may ever receive."

These were the opening words of a workshop given by Kato Havas in Kingston, Ontario in 1979. During the time we spent together she communicated ways in which these ideals might be realized.

I was so delighted with her ideals and means for expressing them that I could not contain my joy. My goodness, here was a Hungarian teacher expressing ideals which parallel Suzuki's. Her desire and ability to enrich the lives of all around her through music and teaching — are these not the same as his?

After living in Japan and studying with Suzuki so closely I developed loyalties and bonds of great love and respect for Suzuki. So, it was with some uneasiness that I attended a workshop given by another "Master Teacher." Many times previously, and often during the workshop, I asked myself if I was scorning the teachings of Suzuki by being there. Then I reviewed what I really learned from Suzuki, the deep truths that come through violin and music. I remembered that I felt I knew less after studying a year with Suzuki that before I went to Japan. But I did feel I must study and find out how to express **music**. Indeed, I left Japan as a student, nothing more.

One of my greatest delights was in becoming accustomed to the Japanese style of teaching and living. To be able to appreciate Suzuki from this different level of perception was, and is, a great joy. I still learn and teach from this perspective. I was astonished at such a Western style of teaching when I first tuned in to Kato Havas. But gradually I began to see and feel the wonderful similarities in direction and the wonderful differences in means. To have met and studied with two such people working for the nobility and spirituality of all people is almost too much greatness to soak up.

We all know that Suzuki bases his teaching and style of playing after Fritz Kreisler. But there is much more about Kreisler that Suzuki studied than just how he played the violin. Can you imagine my delight when Kato said, "A gypsy violinist makes you cry, then laugh. If one can follow him through that, no one would need a psychiatrist. Kreisler was a gypsy violinist who could play Bach."

Going In Circles

There is a *Zen* saying that: "A student progresses in direct proportion to how much he loves his teacher."

Recently I found some old newsletters that I had written years ago. I was curious to see what I had written about. I have an odd habit with writing. As soon as I write something, I forget about it. Sometimes I pick up something and read it and wonder if it is some kind of trick. I can't actually believe that I could have written it. I just can't understand where those ideas came from.

Before I went to live in Japan, I was very insecure about my teaching; I didn't have enough technique on the violin and I didn't have the knowledge that is expected of a violin teacher. I felt completely inadequate, especially around someone who was "better prepared" than I.

The book *Nurtured by Love* made me wonder what the important element of teaching really was. Everything in the book pointed to the premise that love was the key element in teaching. I found this idea heart-warming but somewhat hard to believe. How could a man base his teaching on love? I went to Japan to study this question. The answer came very quickly in the presence of Suzuki.

I found my answer in only a few days there, but stayed on long after. I kept on finding out that same answer deeper and deeper all the time. I came to believe that without love there is only surface teaching. With love, everything seems to work properly.

I no longer have those insecurities about my teaching. I no longer need to judge or criticize other teaching. In my heart I am secure in the answer that I found. It doesn't matter if other people think that this is the right answer or not. I am fully convinced about it and secure in that knowledge. As a matter of fact, I have stopped thinking of myself as a violin teacher; I now think of myself as a music teacher.

All of these things tell about where I am now. Can you imagine my surprise when I read a newsletter I had written four years ago and found that I had written the same thing then! I keep thinking that I am making new discoveries, but find that, in reality, I keep rediscovering the same answers and have gone in a circle.

When I found that, I realized that writing newsletters had come full circle for me too. I have reached the beginning point which is the ending point.

This means that this is the last issue of the newsletter because it is the same as the first issue. It is a bit sad in a way, because writing has made me feel close to many people.

I used to think that it was impossibly courageous to base a music teaching method on love. I mean, how can we talk about that in public? I am not prepared to say that I have found the final answer, but I am prepared to say that I have found my answer for now and it works in my music. Thanks for letting me make this circle with you. I can't really tell if this is the beginning of the end or the end of the beginning.

Epilogue: The Gift

One of my joys in life for many years was in giving gifts to people. In Japan this joy turned into a regular part of living. One never visited a friend's house without a gift in hand. Gift giving was as natural as eating.

I guess I had assumed that this custom would follow me to America and stay with me. But somehow the most amazing thing happened to me when I returned. I found it impossible to give gifts. Not only could I not give them upon visiting a friend, I couldn't give them at Christmas or birthdays. The hardest part was that I couldn't understand what I felt; I only knew that it was impossible for me to give gifts the way I was accustomed to and the way everyone around me was used to. I found this a very difficult situation to be in many times. It often made me very depressed and emotional. Still, I knew what I felt, and couldn't bring myself to go against those feelings. Luckily, while I was in Japan, I learned how to wait. Even without understanding what I was waiting for, I knew I had to wait about gift giving.

During my stay in Japan, I had studied *Katsugen Undo*, a Japanese art similar to *yoga*. My *Katsugen Undo Sensei* and Suzuki were good friends and taught alike in many ways. Many lessons that I learned seemed to be because of the ensemble of these two great teachers. During my last week in Japan, I was at a dinner party given by my second *Sensei*. It was a rather melancholy time, because I had grown very close to the other students of the Japanese art, and I loved and respected *Sensei* very much. I knew I would miss them all greatly. I was aware that there were many customs I might break and things that would offend people easily in such a formal and dramatic setting. But my focus was on *Sensei* and I didn't really notice much else.

After we finished eating, the room grew suddenly quiet. I don't know why, but I suspect that *Sensei* had done something that all the students understood very well except me. I sensed the quiet, however, and got very still also. Then *Sensei* began to speak very softly. By this time, after a year, I had begun to sense the profound place that teachers hold in the hearts of Japanese people. I felt an immense amount of love and respect for *Sensei*, but I am sure that mine was nowhere near the level of the Japanese students.

Tabusa *Sensei* began speaking, "In my house I have had a picture of my teacher ever since I left him. It is impossible to get such a picture again, for it was a gift to me by him before he died." That is all I heard, for at that moment he locked eyes with me and gave me that same picture. Time seemed to stop for me. I don't know how long we held that gaze, but I know that when it ended every student in the room was crying. Some were sobbing openly — not so normal in America, but most unusual in Japan. I remember very little after that. I seemed to stay in some kind of timeless state for a long time.

A year later, the connection was made, I realized that the reason I could not give a gift again after that time was that the gift I received from *Sensei* was a gift from so deep that anything else seemed ludicrous. I would never again be able to give a gift that didn't come from the bottom of my being.